Always Right Behind You

Parables & Poems of Love & Completion

Anima Pundeer
& Art Ticknor

TAT Foundation Press

Always Right Behind You:
Parables & Poems of Love & Completion
Copyright © 2021 by Anima Pundeer & Arthur R. Ticknor

All rights in this book are reserved by the authors. No part of the book may be used or reproduced in any manner whatsoever without written permission except in the case of brief quotations embodied in critical articles and reviews.

TAT Foundation Press, Hurdle Mills, NC
Website: *tatfoundation.org*

Cover: Design by Shambhavi Pundir and Stephen D'Andrea

Cover fonts: PT Sans, PT Serif, Printers Ornaments One
Text fonts: Palatino Linotype, Life BT, Printers Ornaments One, Lohit Devanagari, Garamond, Amazone BT

Library of Congress Control Number: 2021933663

Publisher's Cataloging-in-Publication data

Pundeer, Anima and Ticknor, Art.
Always right behind you / written by Anima Pundeer and Art Ticknor.
p. cm.
Includes index.
ISBN 978-0-9864457-7-4

1. Spirituality. 2. Self-Realization. 3. Philosophy. I. Title.

About the Authors

Anima was born in Dehradun, Uttarakhand, India, the oldest child of a family who trace their heritage to Rajput warriors.

Art was born in Saratoga Springs, New York, USA, the second child of a family who trace their heritage back to English pilgrims in the Plymouth Colony.

Anima arrived in Pittsburgh, PA in 1998 as a new bride with her husband while he worked toward a Ph.D. at Carnegie Mellon University. She had acquired an undergraduate degree in India and a master's degree in Canada and had spotted a poster on the CMU campus advertising an upcoming meeting on the topic of Life Goals.

Art had moved from Miami, FL to Moundsville, WV in 1991 and, in 1997, began holding self-inquiry discussion meetings in Pittsburgh with posters scattered around the CMU and University of Pittsburgh campuses.

Anima showed up at a meeting on Life Goals, which she assumed would be about careers but found that the discussion focused on spiritual self-inquiry. Art began the meeting by going around the table asking each person what their major life goal was. Most of the participants had rather vague ideas about theirs. When it was Anima's turn, she heard herself saying that it was to become enlightened in this lifetime, surprising herself and delighting Art to meet a kindred spirit.

We became great friends and co-workers, each reaching our goal around the same time a decade or so later.

Anima now lives in Houston, TX, and Art in Ocala, FL. We have led at least one self-inquiry retreat together most years, and we keep in touch on a frequent basis. Chuck W., a participant at a retreat in 2018, dedicated the following kind and humorous thank-you to us, which may help paint a portrait of our personalities if you don't yet know us:

I wanted to thank you both for the retreat. I was inspired in many ways not the least of which was seeing selfless generosity expressed through the both of you. I know it takes time, money and lots of energy to contribute to a retreat and for that gift I am grateful. I am also thankful for:

Art's deepening openheartedness
  Anima's deep love and concern for Art
    Art's reckless abuse of ice cream and burnt coffee
      Anima's authentic transparency around the experience of her mother's death
        Art's frustration with those of us who stand in the middle wanting it both ways
          Anima's ferocity that obviously comes from something or somewhere greater than herself
            Art's wisdom combined with an extraordinary depth of knowledge
              Art and Anima's humility
                The Light that shines through you both…

Photo from a women's retreat in 2007. Prior to that, all our retreats had been for both men and women. After that, the men decided they had to have their own retreats. So we continued the three varieties of retreats for several years then gradually moved back to having only retreats for both women and men.

Reviews, Pertinent and Impertinent

We asked some of our friends and authors of TAT Foundation Press books to take a look at the first chapter of this book ("Where to Begin") and provide their impressions for future readers.

❧

Many of us struggle with how to move, how to find that first step within. What can I do to find my truth, my own path to understanding, a point of entry? This book is that point. Forged in friendship, and written from an intimate understanding of the human dilemma, *Always Right Behind You* is an open window on higher wisdom. A guidebook can help us, sometimes in joy, sometimes in sorrow, to take that first step into ourselves. Let this book help you in taking those first steps on the trail within.

~ Bob Fergeson, author of *The Listening Attention; Dark Zen: A Guru on the Bayou;* and contributing author of *Beyond Mind, Beyond Death.*

❧

Whether this is the first book about the nature of human life and existence that you have come across or the thousandth, you're in for a treat. Woven between the threads of Art and Anima's friendship and spiritual journeys are snippets of wisdom, provocative questions and honest stories, all in the name of sharing this most profound and rewarding aspect of life. What a lovely book!

~ Tess Hughes, author of *This Above All: A Journey of Self-Discovery.*

❦

I just finished the first chapter. "Where To Begin," from Anima's and Art's new book, *Always Right Behind You.* Well, I'll begin by saying this pairing of writings by Anima Pundeer and Art Ticknor is proof that the Whole is greater than the sum of the parts! Anima's forceful, heartfelt insights, and directness in telling the simple truths about how people live their lives, plus Art's practicality, clarity, insight, depth of focus and precision in describing the paradoxes in how people live their lives, equals a compelling and inspirational message that evokes the seriousness a spiritual path deserves and requires, and leads the reader's attention in the only direction where real truth and self-realization can be found—inward.

~ Bob Cergol, contributing author of *Beyond Mind, Beyond Death* and working on *HOPE! Life's Calling and the Quest for Identity.*

❦

And this review is from a friend who volunteered to edit the book for us:

This is a beautiful, honest, heartfelt and resonant collection, filled with many kinds of writing—essays, poems, interviews, stories, correspondences, and so much more—that traverse and transcend cultures, countries and centuries. No matter what kind of seeker you are, I am confident that you will find something here to pull you in and deepen your relationship with the Absolute. I found this book engrossing and had to constantly stop, re-read and mull over the truths that the authors point us toward with simplicity, humor, encouragement and caring. In *Always Right Behind You*, Art Ticknor and Anima Pundeer generously invite the reader to become part of their family—the timeless, universal family of seekers—and I for one am delighted to accept this invitation.

~ Chitra Banerjee Divakaruni, author, poet, and the Betty and Gene McDavid Professor of Writing at the University of Houston Creative Writing Program. Her short story collection *Arranged Marriage* won an American Book Award in 1996, and two of her novels *(The Mistress of Spices* and *Sister of My Heart)*, as well as a short story, *The Word Love,* were adapted into films.

Table of Contents

1 Where to Begin 14
    Gayatri Mantra 15
    Gurus 17
    The Summer of 1998 18
    Always Right Behind You 21
    Opening a Path 23
    A Simple Formula 25
    Questions from Mark 26
    Direct Experience 31
    Guru-Shishya 33
    Apple Tree 36
    Decalogue. 37
    Why Stories? 39

2 Suffering 42
    Renouncing Maya 43
    The Horse Is Out 44
    Is It Worth It? 45
    Longing 46
    Poison Ivy. 47
    Separation Anxiety. 49
    Witnessing Death 50
    Seriously 53
    Monody 57
    Shades of Gray 58
    Ordinary People 59
    Love Is Simple 67
    Nature 68
    The Ascent of Mount Carmel 69

	The Love Beyond Love 70
	Enlightenment Holds 71
3	Walking the Path 73
	Thy Will 74
	Dream Comfort 76
	Pass It On 78
	Teacher Criteria 80
	Desire vs. Longing 81
	What Tool to Use 82
	Notes from a 1981 Winter Intensive 83
	In Memoriam: Douglas Harding 86
	Feedback to Art 89
	Wakil's Dream 90
	Struggling Blindly 92
	What Seekers Can Learn from Sikhism: The Path of Service 93
	Strategy 95
	I Don't Get It 98
	Time Capsule 99
4	Self-Inquiry 102
	First Glimpse of Home 103
	Let Death Be Your Teacher 104
	Opening Your Heart 107
	Rapport 109
	When Confrontation Works 110
	Salvation 112
	Silence 113
	I Believe That.... 114
	Facing Fear & Depression 116
	Nuts and Bolts 119
	Nostalgia 128
	Turning Attention from Not-Self 130

And God Smiled	132
Does the Mind See?	138
Overwhelmed	140
Evolution of a Seeker	142
5 Identity	**146**
Slippery Eel	147
Self-Definition	150
Process Observer	152
Promise	154
Maniram's Pets	155
Loss of Self	160
The Ego	162
How Do You Relate to Me?	165
Dead Particles	166
Elusion	167
Homage to Love	168
Feet of Clay	169
Productive Mood	170
Purpose and Benefit	172
Tough Love	174
6 Is There an End?	**175**
When Flame Was a Flower	176
Buddha Nature	179
Where Is the Path?	180
The Nature of Desire	183
Complete Surrender	186
O Come, All Ye Faithful	188
Craving, Longing, Yearning	189
Understanding the Mind	190
Emotions	192
Loss of Everything	193
No Room	194

1
Where to Begin

Gayatri Mantra

The Gayatri Mantra is an ancient sacred hymn from the *Rig Veda*, the oldest[1] of the four Vedas. It is in Sanskrit, dedicated to Savitur, the sun god, who represents the physical and the divine in all things.

ॐ भूर् भुवः स्वः ।
तत्सवितुर्वरेण्यं
भर्गो देवस्य धीमहि।
धियो यो नः प्रचोदयात् ॥

oṃ bhūr bhuvaḥ svaḥ
tat savitur vareṇyaṃ
bhargo devasya dhīmahi
dhiyo yo naḥ prachodayāt
– Rigveda 3.62.10

There are hundreds of translations and explanations for this mantra. The literal meaning is somewhat:

> Om, the Brahm, the Universal Divine Energy, vital spiritual energy (Pran), the essence of our life existence, Positivity, destroyer of sufferings, the happiness, that is bright, luminous like the Sun, best, destroyer of evil thoughts, the divinity who grants happiness may imbibe its Divinity and Brilliance within us which may purify us and guide our righteous wisdom on the right path.[2]

---

1   Written between 1800-1500 BCE.
2   Meditation on the Gayatri Mantra, by Pt. Shriram Sharma.

Where to Begin

I was about 4 years old when my aunt taught me this mantra. Along with the Sanskrit words, she also taught me the meaning in Hindi, which I recited like a parrot. The meaning that she taught me was rather simplistic: "O Protector, Bliss-giver, the one who is as dear to me as my Prana,[3] I am thinking of/ contemplating your beautiful luminous brilliance. Please take my mind towards you."

My entire life I recited this mantra whenever I wanted to say an official prayer or I was in a fix and needed to make an appeal to the higher power for help. Never did my attention go towards what the words really meant. One day, just out of the blue, I noticed the deep meaning behind these simple words. I realized that it is an expression of love and gratitude towards the Source, the Braham,[4] and a plea for help to turn my wandering mind towards it.

It made me think of how man has hungered to know his Source ever since that early time period, where we have documentation of what was going on in his intellectual arena. The obstacles of man in 1800 BCE weren't very different from the man of the 21st century. The mind, the essential tool required to know the Absolute, was perceived as a problem in man's journey inwards, as its nature is to wander off in an outward direction. It surprised me how aware man was of his limitations that long ago. He felt the need for divine intervention to control his mind and did not hesitate to pray for help.

~ Anima

---

3 Breath, Life Force
4 Brahman (the more common Sanskrit form): the Absolute, the Unmanifested Source; as distinct from Brahamaa (Bru-hu-maa), the god of the primary Hindu trinity responsible for creation.

Gurus

In the *Bhagavad Gita*, when Arjuna, the warrior-prince, is torn over his duty to fight an invading army when he sees it includes family members and friends, Lord Krishna tells him that it is He, not Arjuna, who determines what happens.

When the student is ready to hear the ring of truth, the guru appears, with the job of directing the seeker to look within.

Anima's father and uncle were devotees of Rajneesh, later known as Osho. Her dad would take the kids to the local Osho Ashram on the weekends. There was always great food, and meditation with music. This is where she was introduced to different techniques of meditation. Osho's books and talks also helped her understand her own psychology.

Art was in his early 30s when the guru, in the form of Richard Rose, appeared to him at the meeting of a self-inquiry discussion group at Ohio State University in Columbus, OH. As he heard Richard Rose talking, a gong sounded inside Art, accompanied by the thought: "This man is speaking the truth. I've never heard it before, but there's something in me that recognizes it."

That encounter in 1978 set Art on a conscious path of going within to find Truth and, following Rose's advice, finding other seekers to work together with. He was still pursuing the goal when Anima met him and became a fellow seeker.

Where to Begin

Just like when you go on a trek, and the peak looks really afar, you keep taking one step at a time, trudging along, while keeping an eye on the mountain top. The journey may seem hard and impossible, but you just have to keep taking one small step at a time.

~ Anima

Always Right Behind You

Not as in behind your body but as in no matter how fast you look back at where you've just been looking out from, you don't see anything. It's as if what you are moves back behind you as soon as you try to see it, regardless of whether you're looking outward or looking back.

Until we find ourselves at the source of our being, we believe we're something "out here" in the world, part of the cosmos. But the cosmos and that out-here us may be like a giant hologram... shadows from light projected from some unknown source through some unknown transparent template or, in low tech terms, shadows on the wall in Plato's Cave.

The body-us is surrounded by the rest of the cosmos. Our essence or essential self is the source of the light of awareness that creates the cosmos. We have to travel back through the mind, back along the ray of creation, to find our way Home. It sounds like a daunting if not impossible process, but it happens when the conditions are right.

Life works to loosen the illusory beliefs we have about what we are. I felt strongly that there was unseen help in setting up the conditions that loosened the keystone in the arch of my faulty beliefs. Richard Rose, my primary teacher and guru, said in a 1978 public talk[5] at Ohio State University:

> I believe that everybody has a guardian angel. I don't think this is fiction. I believe everybody has a guiding spirit. In fact I've often said that behind all my searching

---

5   Transcript in the June 2020 *TAT Forum*, https://tatfoundation.org/forum2020-06a.htm#6/.

and struggling, there are many things that happened in my lifetime that I could not in my computer have rigged. There were situations I didn't even want to get into, but that I found out later were for the best. So I get the feeling that back behind the curtain there's an intelligence pulling my wires which is for the best.

I don't have a conviction about guardian angels, but I do feel there's both help and hindrance, seen and unseen, along the path to self-realization. And I suspect that a commitment to help others may affect the help that we receive.

The mirror where self sees itself is right behind you.

~ Art

Opening a Path
Shawn Nevins[6]

I am opening a path for you.
Listen to these words.
From where are they coming?
Where do they go in the silence after this sentence?
Look into your mind. The_next_word_is_here.
You observe these words—so too does your neighbor.
Actually look at your neighbor. There is something in them,
which is in you.
Now turn with me and ask, "who is observing?"
Anything you can see is not you.
So how will you define your self?

All of my words miss the mark,
But the answer is within.
Only within is better described as enveloping and surrounding,
Because to go within is to transcend.
You need only listen to the sound of the one hand clapping,
Which dissolves into silence.

Words are dust if they are not felt.

Now choose a memory
(And we won't address the question of how much choice you have).

---

[6] See more of Shawn's poetry in the *TAT Forum* archive (https://tatfoundation.org/forum_indexSNpoetry.htm) and in TAT Foundation Press books such as *Hydroglyphics: Reflections on the Sacred, Images of Essence,* and *Beyond Mind, Beyond Death.*

Questions from Mark

Mark: I'm curious about a couple of things; When you realized the Pittsburgh group meetings were not about how to become successful in life, were you pleasantly surprised, interested, what?

Anima: A little disappointed that it wasn't the career-oriented group, because I really needed help about what could I do that I would 'enjoy' and also help pay my bills. But I was ecstatic, totally thrilled, to find this set of people that were ready to talk and hear me about the subject I was really interested in… MYSELF :).

M: Why did you stick around, and how did this path feel in contrast to your spiritual pursuits in India? Even generally, what kind of preconceptions did you have about the idea of participating in a "spiritual" group in the US? For example, how could anyone in the US know anything about Zen, etc.? In retrospect, in what ways do you think Art helped you? A few examples would be helpful.

A: You wouldn't have been able to keep me away even if you wanted to. I saw the group as directed solely towards self-discovery. Week after week, with each topic, I felt I was getting to see aspects of myself I would otherwise never have considered on my own. It was as if for the first time in my life, I actually started to become aware of my sleepy state. I learned to live an examined life.

The group did not fit my paradigm of spirituality. There wasn't any discourse about God, or prescribed practices. There was no Guru on a pedestal, or photo of a holy man/god/deity with flowers and incense sticks. No robes, no security guards, no waiting lines, no halls, and no monetary transaction involved.

I had tried to find a local spiritual group in Pittsburgh. There was a *Geeta*[7] study group where everyone knew what Krishna is teaching Arjuna. It seemed like people just wanted to show how knowledgeable they were. There was also a Buddhist group, which was mostly about rituals and right practice. I still went to the Hindu temple with a very cynical attitude, mostly for food. I was just plain stupid and arrogant.

The Pittsburgh Philosophical Self-Inquiry (PSI) group didn't seem like a spiritual group but more of a philosophical, psychological, introspective group to me.

One of my favorite questions that got asked was, "Are you a robot?" Though my first response was of course not... "I am not a robot because I am aware of myself," but on close examination in the following weeks, I noticed my actions, reactions, the choices I made, my life was completely mechanical... I couldn't even see which 'self' was really aware.

Going to the meetings was very deflating for the ego. It is hard on the ego to see its projections get punctured constantly. Pretty soon I realized it is best to just shut up and watch other people make a fool of themselves. There is no right answer when it comes to Art, the monitor of the meeting. It was much easier to win arguments with him in my head.

Reading Mr. Rose was equally torturous. What did he mean by creating tension to propel the organism? Meditate on your humiliations vs. meditation that puts you in that placid state of mind? Doubt everything except your ability to doubt? Become your own authority?

This group was a complete contrast to my very eastern state of mind. Looking at my motives behind actions wasn't really a part of my psychology.

---

7   *Bhagavad Gita*

Where to Begin

Though Mr. Rose was not teaching anymore and had an advanced stage of Alzheimer's, I could feel his presence in the way all his students talked about him. There still is a very strong bond based on gratitude and awe towards him, which is still quite evident amongst his students.

M: Did you think your days of following a spiritual path were over when you got married, moved to Texas and started having children, and did you think that when you moved to the US?

A: Yes, I did. Life of a householder meant duties and responsibilities that would take me away from my spiritual path. I even contemplated running away and becoming a nun at some point. But then I realized that no matter where I go, there I will be. The suffering was coming from within. I am the one who is projecting this painful universe. The same universe would appear no matter where I would go. Outside is only mirroring what is inside.

Looking back, there is not a single hair that was out of place in my life that did not contribute towards my spiritual goals.

Moving to the US was sort of a liberating experience for me. At least I did not need to constantly struggle to keep compliance with my social roles. Away from my village, I was a nobody… there were no expectations from outside or inside, and that was a very freeing experience.

M: Did Rose's system resonate with you, and in what sense did you make your path your own? In retrospect, was there a particular point in time when that happened, and did you realize it at the time?

A: I tried really hard to figure out what exactly was Mr. Rose's system. I was looking for instructions to follow. The human condition is such that we would rather be told what to do than figure out what we need to do. We worship authority. It is much easier to be a servant than to be a master. I think that is why Mr. Rose said "Become your own authority."

His talks on the human condition, nature, psychology, helped me to understand the organism anima. It brought clarity to my thinking about my real motives behind my actions. His system really proves itself just as he says.

Fellow seekers in the PSI Group and the TAT Foundation helped to intensify my desire for Truth. Mr. Rose says that what helped him, though he talks about Zen a lot, was his inner determination. He said, "leave no stone unturned." It was no longer a game played in life, but life lived to play the Master Game.[8] He showed the Way.

In spite of having big goals, I really had no idea what to do, so I just became Art's shadow. Whatever he did, I tried to copy him. If he said he sits in his chair and meditates in the morning, I meditated (or tried to figure out what exactly is meditation, how to do it); if he went for solitary "isolation" retreats, I had to do it, too. Learning happens through osmosis; most of my pretenses, my dysfunctionalities, fell off just by being around Art. I tried to get my external and internal house in order, which is a dynamic, ever-changing process. At some point, you just have to decide what is good enough. Please do not ask if my house is in order now. It is still a work in progress.

The path unfolds. You just can take one step at a time. Depending on what you perceive as the immediate obstacle, you take the required action while keeping your attention on what your goal is.

---

[8] Referring to Robert S. de Ropp's book *The Master Game*. See www.selfdiscoveryportal.com/arMasterGame.htm/.

in a rip tide, which I'd never heard of, off Redondo Beach in southern California, flailed until my arms and legs wouldn't work any longer, accepted death & relaxed (to my surprise). I lost body consciousness and saw a life-review before coming back to consciousness a good distance up the beach. The third time was in 2004, when "ego death" occurred. The term is paradoxical, since the sense of being a separate self doesn't die, but our identification with it dissolves.

It's amazing how much suffering we "demand" before being moved to acceptance and then from acceptance to a final surrender—acceptance of what we're not and surrender to what we are.

God the True Mother-Father is always saying: "Come home & all will be well." We hear it when we turn our attention to our deep longing. We court distraction, though, intuiting that we're not yet ready. As Richard Rose's stepdaughter said to him after she read *The Albigen Papers*, "I know you're God, Daddy... but I still have games to play." When we're ready to respond to the call of our deep longing with all our heart, we find the way.

I hope the above communicates a mood that's a possible precursor to what you're looking for.

~Art

Guru-Shishya

The word Guru means one who dispels darkness. One who brings clarity to what my real identity is, is a Guru, a teacher. According to the Hindu Vedas and Buddhist scriptures, to get a human body is extremely rare, to have spiritual thirst is even rarer, and then to find a perfect Teacher is the greatest blessing one can have. Moksha (liberation) comes by Guru's grace.

※

Do we need a teacher on our spiritual journey?

A seeker who has become relatively serious about his search realizes that there really is no predictable path. Is it necessary that your teacher must be enlightened? One who can see me a little better than I see myself, is my Guru.

We are always looking for a teacher, in temples, books, teachings, people who we think have made it. I found that whatever point I was at, there was a teacher outside to show me the next turn. Outer Guru is only mirroring your inner Guru. As Ramana Maharishi said, "Guru is none other than the Self. As the seeker's mind is bent outward, the self takes a human shape as a Guru, to help drive it inwards."

Guru does not make you Enlightened. He helps you get rid of your ignorance. It is your focus and inner resolve that help you reach your goal. Guru only shines the light and nudges you on a path. Being in the presence of a Guru intensifies your desire for Truth. Learning happens not through hearing but through osmosis. You learn through observing your teacher.

How do you find a teacher?

As the saying goes, when the student is ready, the teacher appears.

If you are in a big hall and see a man sitting on a pedestal, lecturing a big crowd, paying for his lifestyle through your pocket, I would recommend getting away from there as soon as you can. He may be a good speaker, and you may buy into his spiel, but it wouldn't be more than that. If there is a system being taught, a certain way of lifestyle preached, then by its very nature, it cannot work. You get busy with working the system or living a certain way of life. You may lose a lot of years and money by the time you realize what a fool you have been. Or maybe it helps because it is your inner journey and what will work as your key can't be predicted. Just be cautious, dear fellow seeker.

Guru-shishya Relationship[9]

In Indian tradition, students would go and live with the Guru in their ashram till Guru gave them permission to go back into the world and live their life. The student would approach the Guru with twigs in his hands, signifying contribution to the fire-wood for the kitchen. Probably it was like an immersion program of our time. Students learned all facets of life from living with the teacher. Guru is an infinite resource of teaching, healing, and guidance. Guru is the source of inspiration and guidance that helps you become your highest potential.

---

9   Teacher-student.

I found that my teacher did not have any other motive but to help me with whatever I was having a problem with at any point in time. And as we all know, there is no dearth of problems in life. I sought answers for mundane problems more than my spiritual problem. I am amazed at how much patience he must have had to tolerate my constant complaints about life, god and other humans.

Each one of us is unique and different and comes with our very special obstacles (so we think). The teacher does not impose his way of thinking but pokes you to think for yourself. I never got a straight answer from my teacher but a question as a response. Guru provides that extra heat that helps the fruit to ripen faster.

The Guru-shishya relationship is very unique. It cannot be compared with any other relationship. Guru is like a flowing river. It doesn't mind how much water you draw out of it. There is always much more than you can take. It depends on the student, how thirsty he is, and how empty his vessel is.

Shishya, to be able to learn, has to surrender his pride. He has to learn to listen with an open heart and mind. All seekers should have one Krishna in their life who they can love and respect and listen to, even when they do not agree. It is not the Guru but faith in the student's heart that holds the magic of transformation.

Where would I be if I hadn't met my teacher! I finally understand when Kabir[10] says that "Guru and Govind (God) both are standing in front of me, who shall I bow to first? I am eternally grateful to my Guru who has shown me the way to Govind."

Guru is found by the grace of God and God is found by the grace of the Guru. Guru and Govind are not two.

~ Anima

---
10   15th Century mystic from India.

8. The biological role / natural purpose of the female is to bear children and be submissive to the male. The role of the male is to protect the female and children.
9. Sociologists and psychologists are building a paradigm full of lies. Most psychologists since (and including) Freud (but excluding Jung) have been packagers or marketers.
10. All you need to do is to listen to the conflicting voices within yourself.

~ Art

Why Stories?

Storytelling is central to human existence according to anthropologists. Through stories, we try to share our experiences of life with each other. Our perspective of the world, of life, gets shaped by the stories we hear, read and share.

Stories have been an integral part of my life. My first memories are of listening to stories that were told by my grandmother. I lived with my grandmother for the initial years of my life because my mom was finishing her degree. There was a story of a thirsty crow, another of a lion and a rabbit, and my most favorite, the story of two birds who are only found in the mountains and make a particular sound. The story was that the bird died before the fruit ripened. So its soul flies in the mountains wailing, "Kophal (the fruit) ripened but I didn't taste it". Every evening it was the repetition of the same set of stories.

My mother was really a good storyteller as well. I remember in summer all of us slept on the terrace, under the stars. Did you know that the north star is not a north star but it is Dhruva, a little boy who found the Father of the whole Universe by praying when he wasn't allowed to sit on the lap of his worldly father. The seven stars in Orion are the seven great Rishis. They are eternal because they found Moksha.

Stories from the *Mahābhārata* and *Rāmāyaṇa* epics got the complete attention of my little brain. Characters and scenes would come to life in my imagination. But my most favorite of them all was Krishna. His personality is such that it is hard not to love him and consider him a friend. I remember getting nightmares where I was chased by my versions of ghosts and demons, and I would call Krishna for help. Sometimes I

Where to Begin

would wake up and would try to keep my mind focused on Krishna to not let any dream demons creep up on me.

We lived in a small village and didn't have much access to libraries, but my grandfather's bookshelves had a lot of esoteric books. Some of them had interesting pictures of deities and demons. I remember very vividly a full-page colorful scene of a Narak,[11] where men and women are getting burnt, getting poked by big shovels. I guess religion serves a purpose of keeping humans aligned to do the right thing by creating the reward and fear of heaven or hell.

Our school library had a fairly good collection of children's storybooks. I would find myself becoming Alice and getting transported to the wonderland. No matter how many times I would hear, read, or think about the story of Mary and Jesus, my heart would feel a tinge of sadness.

I remember trying to understand God who is all-powerful, all-knowing, and all-present, without any shape or form, when I heard the story of Nachiketa, a boy who followed the God of Death, Yama, to know the Absolute Truth. My little mind couldn't understand this formless God and kept bugging my mom with questions. Finally, she said "Just like air that we can't see but is there all around, God is also all around but we can't see. And since God has no shape or form, It will become anything that I imagine and will appear when I remember him with a pure heart." I got this idea that if I really concentrated on this image of God that I created in my mind, It would appear. Should I imagine It as a fish, but then It will need water; or a flower, but then how will It talk? So I stuck to my image of Krishna. Ever since then I have had a very special relationship with Krishna.

With teenage years, my separate self got stronger. Stories of wonderment got replaced by the reality show of

---

11 Hindu equivalent of Hell.

life… drugs, booze and dance. Just kidding! The story of 'my life' took precedence ever since then. I became the main character, always taking the center stage in 'my' life drama.

Dear reader, I hope you can read these stories with a childlike curiosity and wonderment, with an open mind. Our intent is that you get to see something about yourself through these stories from near and far, stories of human suffering, of pride, of Love, of Completion.

~ Anima

The Horse Is Out

The horse is out of the barn,
 The parrot got out of the cage,
Some unintended behavior pattern manifested…

If you're the horse, you're undoubtedly happy about it
If you're not the horse, you may or may not be happy:

If you are, then there's no problem from your perspective
If not, you may determine to circumvent a future repetition.

Some people get discouraged
And give up before they even get started
While others manifest a repetitive on-again, off-again pattern:

Acquiring self-definition or becoming self-realized
May require tremendous strain and effort before the
Effortless phase of continued effort without trying kicks in.

Why becoming what you already are, have always been, and
Ever will BE requires so much "doing" is a paradox to make
The angels weep… to borrow a phrase from Alfred Pulyan.

~ Art

Is It Worth It?

Someone once asked me if, in the end, all this seeking is worth it.

I had to think about it as this thought had never crossed my mind before. I realized that knowing what I know now, I wouldn't be able to take any other path. Suppose there were two roads I could choose from, one leading to heaven and the other to hell… where heaven meant eternal life of no pain or suffering, only pleasure, the best of foods, wines, music, dances or whatever my imagination can associate with heaven; and the road to hell meant suffering and pain all around, getting thrown into the fire, getting poked by knives and swords and whatever else that imagination can conjure up with hell, but this would be the only way for me to find the Truth—I would choose to go through this passage of hell.

All pleasures eventually become suffering. Even eternal life in heaven cannot resolve the inner angst emanating from the separation from your Source.

~ Anima

Longing
Ben Rainey

Call me to You, oh my Source.
Let me stumble into You, losing my self.
How can my pride compare with Your Beauty?
How can my weakness stray from Your Love?
My fears run away from You
And my desires overlook You,
Yet where are You not?
Make me to know Your ever-presence,
And allow me to rest in the Eternal arms of Your Love.
Call me to You, oh my Source.
Swallow me whole, and dissolve me in Completion.

Poison Ivy

I am convinced that even if I think of poison ivy, my skin will break into blisters! The sap of the poison ivy plant, also known as Toxicodendron radicans, contains an oil called urushiol. This is the irritant that causes an allergic reaction and rash. Coming in contact with this plant causes red itchy rashes which are painful. My skin also gets blistered with liquidy stuff in it. Not a pleasant sight at all.

It was the summer of '99. A work weekend was planned at the Richard Rose farm. We were to trim the bushes and clean the walkways. I had no idea of the existence of poison ivy then. Or of its impact on the human body. Sure enough, in the evening, when we got back home, I noticed my leg had a red rash. My left arm also felt really itchy. The itch pretty soon turned into a burning sensation, then huge blisters that covered my hand and my leg appeared. It lasted about three weeks but felt like a lifetime of sheer torture. I couldn't think or do anything else but constantly had my attention on my blisters while they lasted.

I realized that the nature of life isn't very different from the nature of poison ivy. Life experiences draw my attention continuously outwards. Depending on the direction of the wind, the experiences feel pleasurable or painful, but in any case, they are completely engaging. Unless some aspect of your life experience makes you want to turn your attention away from it, why would you question it? For a dreamer to realize he is dreaming, something in the dream has to poke the dreamer. I am very thankful that my life was providing me with ample pokes. However, no matter how I tried to turn

Suffering

my attention away, it remained on the scene. The perceived content of it, though, changed.

I understood then what Mr. Rose meant by "You back into Truth."

~ Anima

Separation Anxiety

I heard a lovely woman say
I cried every single day
of kindergarten. I just
wanted to be home, with
my mother. Not even my
older brother, who the teacher
brought into the room
to comfort me, could ease the
misery of separation.

~ Art

Witnessing Death

I was 12 when my 7-year-old cousin fell off the stairs, got a brain hemorrhage, and died. It happened in the big, ancestral home where my uncle's family and we lived. When I got back from school, I was told that she was taken to the hospital. She had tripped while sliding off the railing of the stairs onto the concrete floor of the courtyard. She didn't have any physical wounds, but she had a blue bruise on the side of her head. In the evening, all the kids got to go to the hospital to meet her. She lay in bed with an IV needle in her little hand, was very thirsty, and kept asking for water. Nurses, for some reason, only gave her ice. The next morning I woke up to the sound of my aunt weeping. My cousin had died that night. Her little body, on the floor of our living room, was covered with a white sheet. Someone mentioned that since she was a child, she would be buried and not cremated. I had this sick feeling in my stomach.

That day I realized the finality of death. Also I came to the conclusion of the unpredictability of Yama's[12] arrival. None of the answers about what happens after death was convincing. My little mind wanted to believe that there is an Atman that moves on, changes the body, you go to heaven, you are with God, you become a star. None of these answers felt convincing or reduced that stomach ache.

That same year my grandfather, my mom's dad, passed away. I saw my grandmother and my mother grieve. Death wasn't something that I only heard about; it was experienced in close quarters for the first time. I realized it comes when it wants to, and no one can do anything about it. Something

---

12 God of Death

in you changes when you witness death. Death has a finality to it. I concluded that what is born will die... and I will also die. The idea of my own death didn't feel scary, though. However, the thought that my grandmother will die was a real nightmare for me. I couldn't get rid of it. I imagined that even if she died, I would like to at least keep her body. To this, she laughed and said the body is nothing but mud and needs to get recycled.

In the recent past, I have had to witness some of my close relatives die. I had this idea in my head that dying is the last opportunity as human beings to find liberation from this cycle of birth and death. The only condition would be that your attention finally turns away from this duality, life, and turns towards the Source. As we stand to face death, there is a chance that you can see beyond the fear. I thought that it would be natural for a human being to finally turn away from self and the story. This does not seem to be the case as I saw my relatives on their deathbeds. It surprised me that, even when a man sees that he is nearing his end, the attention remains engaged in the world. Though the body starts to shut down, the mind wants to hold on to the attachments. There was a concern about the next meal, about that last piece of jewelry, about property. My mom, just like my grandmother, the practical skeptic householder that she always was, had a saree picked out that she wanted to get cremated in.

It feels like life-long habits, very basic physical instincts take over our thinking completely. There is no scope for any new or different stream of thought to enter consciousness. How you are living right now is exactly how your final moments will be. At least in terms of your inner room, the mind. Your state of mind will not change from its instinctive state. At least that's how it seemed to me. Though I have heard that some people start to see their long-gone loved ones. Buddhists think that we enter a particular bardo depending on our karma.

Suffering

I wasn't there when my dad passed away. He was 59 and had bone cancer. My mom told me that a visitor who had come to meet my dad asked if he was in pain. My dad replied 'only his body is'.

Dayananda Saraswati[13] was in a state of coma in a hospital in Rishikesh. Someone next to his bed was reading the Geeta to him. Even in that state, people noticed that he had a smile and was saying 'wah! wah!' (words to show appreciation, beauty).

My biggest fear was that on my deathbed I will regret that I failed to give my all to the search. Maybe I should have gone and attended that retreat with Harding; I should have tried my best to make my meditation practice more disciplined; I shouldn't have made excuses that it is because of XYZ that I couldn't do ABC, which may have helped; I failed; now I'll have to go through this cycle of suffering again.

This fear of regret provided that essential fuel for my search.

~ Anima

---

13   Swami Dayananda Saraswati was a renowned traditional teacher of Advaita Vedanta, and founder of the Arsha Vidya Gurukulam. Born: August 15, 1930; died: September 23, 2015.

Seriously

I just feel like I don't have what it takes to do this. I don't feel I have any control or ability to keep up with any commitments. I can go to the gym 3 times a week and drive to work in silence. That is about it. I see everyone else with these commitments to meditation and they are putting so much more into this. I just don't feel like I have what it takes. I don't think I can struggle for another 20 years like this either. Its so damn hard. I'm falling back into some really hard times mentally and emotionally and I just don't know if this is possible for me. It feels like I'm trying to hold up the world right now it is just too much.

Have you noticed that everybody has a story they tell themselves about themselves? This is how the mind keeps up the faulty sense of identity, which relies on being special. "I just feel like I don't have what it takes to do this" is an example of the story of being special. Some people harp on telling themselves how they're superior to others, some tell themselves how they're inferior, but it all serves the same purpose.

    I think you're finding yourself in the trap of taking yourself too seriously. So that everything you do or don't do is of immense importance to you. The truth is far different :-). As Richard Rose used to quip to us guys when we were taking ourselves too seriously, "The first hundred years is the hardest." Where's your sense of humor about yourself?? If the sun is going to "come up" tomorrow, it's going to do so without your help or mine :-). Just do what you can do, and laugh at how "important" it is one way or the other.

    And don't let yourself off the hook by faulty comparisons with how you're so much worse off than other people. When

Suffering

we tell ourselves we're doing all we can be doing, we're kidding ourselves. Everyone is capable of doing more than they're doing... more than they have any idea of. S. B., a longtime TAT member who's now disabled with familial spastic paraplegia and has a woman coming in every day to shave him, get him dressed, prepare meals for him, etc., sent the link to a video of a great talk about that by Napoleon Hill, a protégé whom Andrew Carnegie selected to pass on what he'd learned about success. Rose used to say that Hill's book *Think and Grow Rich* had the success formula for any objective that a person wanted to pursue.

If you keep track of the feeling that guides us to what we really want out of life, you'll find yourself doing the things that lead to success at what's important to you. It's your life... do what you really want to do and don't worry about whether other people think you're doing the right things.

Your friend,

The first part of your response seems to me to be in direct opposition to the second. You tell me don't take myself too seriously that what will happen will happen. Then you sent me that link which stresses the keys to success. Where I have the opportunity to take control of my life and get what I want by doing all these "things." This also seems in contradiction to what people say that there is no free will and things happen as they do. I just went to see Bart Marshall talk in Pennsylvania this past Friday, and it really brought me down. All I could think of was his 37 years of searching, and your decades as well. And how much you've both put in. And paradoxically how it requires all this effort but the realization is that you don't put any effort in and there is no "you" to do any of this... How can I be sure on what I'm doing. How can I make an effort if there is no me to do anything. I've never been successful at making commitments. Ever since I can remember I always hated doing things, setting goals, playing sports, working at school... I don't know if I've ever had any commitment that i was able to keep up with. Maybe this is all a story I'm telling myself. But you say don't take yourself too seriously, but work for what you want. That seems to contradict itself so much to me. I don't understand how I can do both. I don't even know how to commit myself to something. This just is so confusing, I'm sorry Art... I appreciate everything you have done and are doing for me. I just feel like a hopeless case even though maybe I'm just creating some story.

1. Don't take yourself so seriously. Think about it anyway....

2. We don't have any way of knowing whether the sun will appear per usual tomorrow or if it will explode, will be diffused by fog or volcanic ash, etc. But we can be pretty sure those consequences aren't under your and my control.

3. We don't have any way of knowing whether we'll do something we plan to do tomorrow, but it would be silly to assume we don't have any influence over what happens—if we believe we do. But it would also be silly not to question our beliefs.

4. Bart and I both believed that our efforts might have been part of the formula for success in self-definition. We have no way of knowing for sure, but I can guarantee you if I had to do it again, I would definitely plan to work at it again.

5. If you want something enough, you'll work for it. And you won't begrudge the effort. Where did you get the belief that what you want out of life isn't worth struggling for?

6. You can't be absolutely sure about anything other than what you are. You eat food all the time without

Suffering

knowing whether it might kill you, don't you? We operate on probabilities.

7. "There's no me" is pure [baloney]. The Real Me is what everyone is looking for, although the vast majority of people don't consciously know that. But they're looking for Unconditional Love or Total Security or Immortality or You-name-it.
8. Is there nothing you love? Do you have everything you love? If not, are you afraid to go for it?
9. You're stuck in a negative loop of thinking. It has become habitual, and you identify it as you / your way of thinking. If you question it—i.e., watch it with a measure of skepticism—you'll get some detachment from it. The belief in being a hopeless case is a form of self-pity that I'm quite familiar with :-). It's nothing more than a defense mechanism for somebody who doesn't want to take any punches. It's a slower, more cautious path.
10. You need a change of interior scenery :-).

There was an episode of the "Numb3rs" TV series a few years ago that had an epic line in it: "If you want to feel better, take a pill. If you want to get right, face the truth." (Advice of a psychologist to a troubled FBI agent.)

~ Art

Monody
Herman Melville

To have known him, to have loved him
    After loneness long;
And then to be estranged in life,
    And neither in the wrong;
And now for death to set his seal—
    Ease me, a little ease, my song!

By wintry hills his hermit-mound
    The sheeted snow-drifts drape,
And houseless there the snow-bird flits
    Beneath the fir-trees' crape:
Glazed now with ice the cloistral vine
    That hid the shyest grape.

Shades of Gray

The mind triangulates its way over contradictions to a final contradiction. But the mind is a very vague dimension, and the mind-us has to contend with its vagueness all along the way. We are like blind men seeking their way in an infinity of vagueness. We hear voices calling: "this way," or "not that way." Something in us judges how to respond to the conflicting voices, and we move or don't move accordingly.

~ Art

Ordinary People

I used to think of Shawn Nevins as a wandering monk. He would stop by once in a while when he was traveling from one city to another. If we were having a retreat at the farm or in Pittsburgh he would participate. Sometimes he also held a session or gave a presentation. During one of his visits, when he was still seeking, he gave a presentation on meditation and self-inquiry. The statement that got my complete attention was he said that he was at the point where he is quitting meditation. I at once thought now Shawn has no chance of ever getting Enlightened. Unless you have mastered meditation, got your mind under complete control, there was no chance of anyone becoming whatever was my idea of Enlightened.

Sure enough in a couple of months, I heard that Shawn Woke up. It just blew my mind. My firm conviction about what leads us to Enlightenment got completely punctured. After my initial shock, I found a slight hope for myself. Shawn had this persona of being aloof, not talking too much, not overly friendly. I had to gather all my courage, decided to write to Shawn and ask for help.

When someone speaks less we have to pay attention to what they say.

And this is how it went...

August 2001
Anima wrote:

Hi Shawn,
Yesterday, out of the blue, a thought (read it inspiration) crossed my mind and I was really surprised… 'I should make a commitment of writing to Shawn (everyday?)'… actually, I really have not much to say but I thought I'll give it a shot. So if you get emails from me regularly, don't get bugged… just ignore them.

Actually most of the time I keep feeling that I am not trying/desiring /wanting the answers bad enough and I am not 'doing' anything much. So writing to you came as to what I need to be doing at this point.

You know how sometimes you get more intuitive and 'holy' compared to other days when you just are a creature crawling away… so these are my days of being more spiritual. Yesterday I had a real good meditation. After the initial period of rambling thoughts about the different activities of the day… mind got quieter. That felt good. But there is nothing so far that I have found that means going-inwards. I feel the nature of the mind is to look outwards and I wonder if I can turn it inwards on my own.

Thanks a lot for listening… let me know if you find my emailing annoying… my feelings won't be hurt.

in friendship…
Anima

From Shawn:

"Mind got quieter." And then what? What was there? Still outward pointing, or on pause? Looking, listening, or feeling something?

- Shawn

Anima wrote:

Most of the time when the mind becomes quiet... slowly the next thought creeps up. Mind on its own, I think, just sort of waits passively. A few times I got a feel for deep, dark silence which was right there but it was fleeting and for all you know may just have been the creation of my hyperactive mind.

I am trying to make the most of my inspired mood these days... so I have been really good. Did my walking, meditation, and even reading. I got this book, *Instructions to the Cook: A Zen Master's Lessons in Living a Life That Matters*, out of the library. So far most of it I could relate to myself. I liked a metaphor about hungry ghosts who are never satisfied with all the food they get... I could see that hungry ghost in me.

The day otherwise went by fast. I like Thursdays a lot.

Alright, Shawn... will probably write to u tomorrow and may see you on Saturday.

anima

Suffering

From Shawn:

The next thought creeps up from where? From where does it originate—can you see/hear/feel the place from where thoughts come? **Looking back through the mind to the source of thought and source of awareness will lead us home**.

- Shawn

❦

Anima wrote:

Thanks a lot Shawn for the pointer. Is the source where thoughts get created also the source of all creation... I wonder...

❦

Shawn's Response:

You wonder.... **If you know, you will know all that is needed.**

❦

Anima wrote:

This is a real Koan that you threw at me... it almost stopped my head. "You wonder.... If you know you will know all that is needed." I am not getting it Shawn...

anima

❦

Shawn's Response:

Do you want to "get it" is the question. Or do you simply believe it would be nice if you got it? Do you see the **precarious position of Anima and her thoughts**?

- Shawn

Anima wrote:

I do want to 'get it' Shawn. I don't think it is any more 'it-would-be-nice-to get-it'. Yesterday we had a company day-out where the whole dept. went out to a ranch. I started to talk to a guy from India who has read a lot of Indian philosophy. Talking to him made me realize a few convictions that I have which I hadn't noticed before. Throughout our life, we grow up hearing stories about various saints and rishis and how they got enlightened. We also grow up hearing that God is in us and everywhere, but to become it we have to follow a particular path, find a guru and do A, B and C. I think somewhere in mind, I don't know where, I have this belief that I am not good enough to be enlightened because I haven't tried hard enough... and it only happens to saints and rishis in the books. It was interesting to see my own convictions and beliefs through somebody else. People from a particular culture do have almost identical programming. Listening to this guy was almost like hearing myself. It is really amazing how identical we all are.

Thank you for listening,
Anima

Suffering

Anima wrote:

You know, Shawn, for the first time in my life I feel my outside world is in good enough order when I don't need to stay occupied with fixing this or that. Not that everything is the way 'i' would like it to be but it really doesn't matter… things are quite alright… my inner world also feels more or less like that. Since there is not much anxiety from the outside… the inner doesn't have that anxious energy that keeps it occupied or seeking. There is this feeling that the picture is not complete yet. Even without this 'I' running the universe, I know nature has programmed everything so perfectly that the sun will come up tomorrow… without 'me' having to do a single thing. So what do I do now… should I be 'doing' something/anything? I feel it is just my ego's needs to stay occupied and important. I just am having all these confusing thoughts today.

Anima

From Shawn:

The ego is all you have. Negate it too soon and you negate the fuel to search for essence. Save your emails for a week and read them at the end of the week. **Somebody is many bodies.**

- Shawn

Anima wrote:

What do you mean by 'Somebody is many bodies? 'I am starting to get into 'be-miserable-make-everybody-else-miserable' mood today. :) It is being carried over by the dreams I kept getting last night where you are trying to do something but nothing gets done. It is really interesting how my mood gets set by the dreams I get at night... and probably dreams get triggered by the hormones in our body... there is really no me in any of this... and still I feel responsible and guilty and everything else.

It is Friday... I will be back in Pgh... will write to you again on Monday.

thanks for listening...
anima

From Shawn:

Just mean that you are in many moods.

Anima wrote:

I was thinking that if there are many people in one body or different moods... what do you do to keep one log burning with all the energy? I think it is really hard... especially for me. Was it ever hard for you?

Anima

Suffering

From Shawn:

"Each day it is a different mood for me. Actually I have kind of nailed how my mood may be over a week. Sometimes it surprises me when I see I am exactly in the same mood as I was about a month back... the chatter/complaints/irritations/energy level... exactly is the way it was. But since I am not a detail person and would like to be more spontaneous... I don't like to keep a detailed log... however observing and watching the cycle repeat itself has helped me not to be too attached to my emotions."

Little wonder it is especially hard for you. If you are in a different mood each day, then you are spontaneous enough — have some pity for those around you :-). **Perhaps you should become a detail person for a period of time. Become a scientist (for a while).**

The other approach is to **listen with all of your heart to the guru** (which may be a person or place, or perhaps even a mental attitude). Still, you must become one in order to listen and this requires discipline (or earnestness, if you don't like that word).

Yes, it was hard for me as I am an ordinary person. Even until the last moment, there were conflicting drives. **We must forgive our weaknesses even as we strain to overcome them.**

Identify that which distracts or hypnotizes you, and learn to avoid it.

- Shawn

Love Is Simple

To love God
You must end your separation,
Which turns out to have been
A dream of separation.
The dreamer doesn't know
His true identity.

The veil lifts
When the last self-lie
Is seen through...
Following an opposing view
That contradicts the last self-lie.

Having climbed the ladder
Of acceptance or disidentification
From that which is experienced,
The plunge into the pool
Of unknowing awaits.

Love is simple.
Simplify.

~ Art

Nature

Nature is a preparation for religion,
But it is not religion.

Religion is a preparation for self-realization,
But it is not self-realization.

Nature shifts the spotlight of separation
To the floodlight of wholeness.

Religion uses belief to generate faith.
Faith promotes doubt and self-inquiry,
The typical precursors of self-realization.

Self-realization or recognition occurs
When the individual self
Becomes a mirror of the Real…
A Self-aware mirror.

~ Art

The Ascent of Mount Carmel
St. John of the Cross

To reach satisfaction in all
desire its possession in nothing.
To come to possession in all
desire the possession of nothing.
To arrive at being all
desire to be nothing.
To come to the knowledge of all
desire the knowledge of nothing.
To come to the pleasure you have not
you must go by the way in which you enjoy not.
To come to the knowledge you have not
you must go by the way in which you know not.
To come to the possession you have not
you must go by the way in which you possess not.
To come by the what you are not
you must go by a way in which you are not.
When you turn toward something
you cease to cast yourself upon the all.
For to go from all to the all
you must deny yourself of all in all.
And when you come to the possession of the all
you must possess it without wanting anything.
Because if you desire to have something in all
your treasure in God is not purely your all.[14]

---

14 St. John of the Cross (trans Kieran Kavanaugh OCD—Paulist Press ISBN 080912839X). Text is available under the Creative Commons Attribution: ShareAlike License, Wikipedia®

The Love Beyond Love

Where we *experience* experience is within the mind.
The world of experience is within the mind.
What everyone wants... Full Satisfaction... is beyond the mind.

Within the mind, all is transient.
The most intense beauty in the mind of experience is ultimately unsatisfying because of its transience.
All experience, if recognized, points us back in the direction of Home.

~ Art

Enlightenment Holds

Enlightenment holds

the promise of permanent happiness.
What you find is your understanding of
the word 'happiness' was incorrect.

the promise of Wholeness.
What you find is that the one who wants this
Wholeness is a bottomless, empty hole.

the promise of eternal bliss.
What you find is the wonderment
about the Painter's genius...
Perfection in All you find.

the promise of the end of suffering.
What you find is bygone memories
tainted with stories.
The hook "I am suffering" that keeps
you centralized in the universe was
after all not that strong.
One look and it fizzled.
Suffering disappeared along with the sufferer.

the promise of liberation from bondage.
What you find is that it was all
a big misunderstanding...
There is nothing that can be
bound, nor liberated.

Suffering

the promise of your True Identity.
What you find is the one who wanted
to know, disappeared
along with all his fears, desires
questions and doubts.

What was this separate, limited, lost thing
looking for itSelf?
Where could it go?

What remains is One
ALONE.

~ Anima

3

Walking the Path

Thy Will

And not my will...
You know you are living this when...

- Each moment feels perfect the way it is...
- You wonder sometimes what sort of tune the Composer is planning next...
- You feel like you are just an empty flute and no matter what note is getting played... you know it has to be the best that can be played out... you 'try to' stay out of the way...
- When the song played is really sad and you don't like it much... and it is causing you a lot of pain and heartache... you still want it to be the best sad song for the Composer to feel...
- There is no more feeling of guilt left within...
- There is no more feeling of responsibility left either...
- You really see that you are simply living your dharma...
- No matter how difficult it may seem but, for most parts, you just find yourself doing the 'right thing' or taking the right road...
- And sometimes when pain becomes a bit too much to take... and we all know how "suffering" is an integral part of the nature of life... you really get mad at "u-know-who"...

- All personal preferences lose their importance... you still insist on getting your coffee exactly the way you like it... ☺ ...
- You still meditate/pray sometimes... but you know it really makes no difference...
- You stop asking...
- You start accepting...
- Whatever life experience is unfolding... you just find yourself living it...
- And as you see yourself dissolve... you start noticing how, it always is "Thy Will"... even when you were thinking it is "my will"... ☺ ...
- And then one day you laugh at yourself of how you used to make such a big deal out for really nothing... ☺ ...

These are just my simple thoughts for my dearest friend H...
And yes, when Love comes knocking at our door... it doesn't wait to ask for our permission... ☺ ...
And stubbornness is nothing but manifested pride...

~ Anima

Dream Comfort

Hey, I had an awesome dream about you last night, and thought I should share. In the dream, I was in my grandmother's house in Romania (the one who died last year) and sitting in the room in which she died, where she and I often used to talk about stuff when she was alive. It was really dark in there and for some reason I was really worried about being there, and not knowing how I got there and why I was there all alone. This awful feeling just descended on me out of nowhere, I'm pretty sure I was crying in my sleep. No reason at all, at least not one that I could recognize. Then you appeared in the room out of nowhere and you put your arms around me, and you covered my forehead with your left hand, and immediately I had that feeling that I would often feel as a little kid, when my mom would rub my forehead to calm me down when I was crying. So as soon as you did that I felt better and I was no longer afraid and freaking out and everything just calmed down. So I just wanted to thank you for making an appearance in my dream, although you probably had no inkling of how helpful you were last night

Dreams are strange phenomena, aren't they. I'm convinced they have intelligent purpose & that the dream-maker uses symbols that are relevant to our psyche and memories.

A possible interpretation: The scene of being alone in your grandma's house, in the room where she died, and in the dark, could represent your conception of death. My appearance in the room "out of nowhere" could indicate what you pick up of my origin… as the precursor to being able to see & accept it as your origin. Putting my arms around you could symbolize reassuring the preconceptual emotional child, who picks up communication by touch. Covering your forehead with my left hand could convey that the misery is in the mental story—i.e., left hemisphere functioning—and that it's soothed by connecting with the right hemisphere.

~ Art

Pass It On

Richard Rose was my first contact with the Genuine. In fact he "rang my bell" the first time we met, as I mentioned earlier. It was as if a brass gong within me, whose existence I hadn't even been aware of, had been struck. The words that formed in my mind were: "This man is telling the Truth. I've never heard it before, but something in me recognizes it."

That something was the sleeping inner man, the intuition, which Mr. Rose had awakened. And an intense joy accompanied the awakening.

A year or so later, as I was leaving Ohio for California, I told him I wished there were something I could do to repay him for all he'd done for me. "That's not the way it works," he replied. "Pass it on."

Since then I've tried to make my life an expression of thankfulness for what he's done for me and many others.

The search for Truth, for the recognition of our essential state of being, requires momentum for a possible long haul. After the initial enthusiasm wears off and we find ourselves in an apparent stalemate, how do we keep going? One of the other memorable comments he made that formed my life-action was: "If you can't inspire yourself, find someone else to inspire."

He was strongly convinced of the value of a person's working with other seekers and helping those on the rung of the ladder below them. While the individual's efforts may be tinged with egotism, the chain of helping and being helped thus formed has a great impersonal beauty and can be instrumental in pushing the seeker beyond the bounds of limitation.

Richard Rose—
an angel, not a saint
a messenger
projected by the Self
thru the viewer,
testifying to the fact
that all answers lie within.

From the August 2005 "TAT Forum memorial issue to Richard Rose, *tatfoundation.org/forum2005-08.htm*

~ Art

Teacher Criteria

You know you have found a Teacher when:

- It doesn't burn holes in your pocket when you need to see him
- He will take two steps towards you when you take a step towards him
- You'll know that helping you is the only interest he has in you
- He will know you and see you better than you know and see yourself
- You'll see the honesty and selflessness
- He will not build/enhance your ego
- You'll have not much argument with what he has to say
- He is available to you when you need him
- He will not hold your hand or try to give you the Answer
- He will point you in a direction
- He will encourage you to walk your own path
- He will help you become your own authority

~ Anima

Desire vs. Longing
Dan McLaughlin

Our poor boats are rocked by desire.
Few boats follow their longing Home.

What Tool to Use

To know the taste of sugar
the tongue is used.
Ears hear the birds chirp.
A cool breeze makes the skin
on my arm tingle.
Heart feels joy and sorrow,
love and hate.
Mind does a good job of
churning thoughts, solving puzzles.

What tool do I use
to know
what makes me alive,
the source of sweetness in honey,
music between the notes?
What makes the fire hot?
What is the source of my thought?

What tool could I use?
Do I need a tool?

Is there a thread I can follow
to go beyond the finite
into the Infinite
Me?

~ Anima

Notes from a 1981 Winter Intensive

*R*ichard Rose conducted two month-long winter intensive retreats, one in 1981 and one in 1982. I wasn't able to attend the first one, but I extracted these notes from material provided by a friend who did:

1. An individual can become the Truth through his own striving and determination. A man can strike out on his own and use the dynamics of his mind, body, and spirit. By projecting determination, desire, and energy, he can reach the goal.

2. Speak out for freedom [from conditioning]; fight against oppression; inspire those who yearn to be free of their chains; courageously free yourself from the yoke of your conditioning.

3. We procrastinate [productive] thinking.

4. Going within doesn't require tension; just let it happen. (It's something new.)

5. The mind works too fast to be able to observe the mechanics.[15]

---

[15] However, there have been several occurrences in my life where I was able to see the mind's operation as in slow motion: the first time observing the decision-making process in great detail; the second time observing the mechanics of thought itself... being able to follow thought streams from inception of a percept hitting the mind to the pinball-like path of that percept bouncing off memories until the next percept hit and the next thought stream followed; and observing the rapid computations of massive amounts of data from memory by the intuition process.

6. Consciousness is electrical—the space between two nerve points.
7. How can a person keep his [self-inquiry] thinking stimulated? Requires a ways-and-means "committee" to form in the mind.
8. Personal intensive retreats: One confirms and creates conviction by action.
9. You have to be willing to die for your top priority.
10. Work for success and the work should be enjoyable.
11. Design a master plan for achieving goals.
12. Meditation/evaluation system: A master plan outlining areas to be evaluated.
13. What are my three top objectives? How am I going to accomplish them?
14. The Albigen System as a science [of self-definition].
15. Systematized inspirational reading.
16. Get contagious with success. (Allow this to happen.) Rejoice in successes.
17. Illusion that there's virtue in our current (placid) state of mind.
18. Mental and physical (i.e., mundane) levels have to progress.
19. Have to find your fellow seekers.
20. There has to be a group plan, based on harmony among objectives.
21. Communicate what you're doing and what the system is... in other people's terms.
22. Exert yourself to the point where you feel good, that you're truthfully applying and exerting energy.

23. Look for commonalities. Cherish and nurture them. Don't harp on or criticize differences.
24. Our minor objectives are definable, actionable. The major one isn't.
25. Try to meet the mind of the other person. Be able to ring bells in people.
26. Once you evolve a complete desire for the Truth, you'll realize that you have to put your energy into it 24 hours per day.[16]
27. Mental torpor is caused by forces of adversity.
28. Don't let yourself be enslaved. Know your body functions and regulate them.
29. Watch ourselves to see the pattern imposed on us. Our personality is only what we're allowed to exude.
30. Put yourself in the position of teaching.
31. Success builds the vector.
32. Become a sincere seeker, attempting to meet other seekers and communicate what you've learned along the way.
33. Our realizations will die if they're not communicated.
34. To find the answer, you must teach. To teach, you have to learn the human language. Disdain, deceit, envy, and other aspects of competition will prevent learning the human language. Realize we're all drops of water in the ocean.

~ Art

---

[16] I can't say that a 24x7 dedication ever developed for me. I think it's good to monitor how we're using our free time to see how we can devote it more productively to our highest objective.

In Memoriam: Douglas Harding
February 12, 1909-January 11, 2007

Douglas and Catherine were kind enough to invite me into their home—well, to be more accurate, to agree to my request to visit them—when I was a stranger from another country wanting to bypass one of their public workshops and spend time one-to-one with Douglas.

I spent several hours (six if my memory isn't exaggerating the turmoil) driving a rented car from Ipswich, England to their home, which was only about twelve miles out from the city. What threw me for a loop were the traffic circles, which I had to approach on the "wrong" side of the road, driving a car with a steering wheel on the "wrong" side and a manual gearshift lever on the "wrong" side. By the time I shot through a few of those circles, I had no sense of compass direction. And I saw many sights over and over before finally locating the B&B a mile down the road from the Hardings' residence. Once there, I parked the car and refused to take another chance on getting lost. The next morning the B&B owner drove back to the rental agency in Ipswich with me following, and I got rid of the car.

On the way back, shortly before lunch, he dropped me off for my first visit with the Hardings. Catherine greeted me warmly at the door of a contemporary-style home that had been designed by Douglas, who had been an architect by profession. Douglas was sitting in a wheelchair in his living room—this was in October 2003, when he was 94, and while he was still ambulatory, he often used a wheelchair for ease of moving around the house. His first words after we shook hands were: "Your job is not to be Douglas Harding or someone else. Your job is to become yourself—your real self."

I spent the rest of that day well into the evening with the Hardings and returned the following day late in the morning. Sometime that afternoon I overheard Douglas, down the hall from the living room, say to Catherine: "He's like one of the family. It feels like we've always known him." I had been thinking almost identical thoughts. It was as if we had become family—or closer than family in the way that sometimes happens in the family of seekers.

On the third and final day of my visit, which was a Sunday, Douglas had invited a few students to come for a mini-workshop. We did several of the experiments in direct seeing that he had developed over the decades, one of which was the tube experiment where two people put their faces in opposite ends of a paper tube while someone goes through a progression of questions on what's being seen from a first-person point of view. Douglas and I shared one of the tubes while he talked through the exercise for those of us present. While he was doing this, I saw very clearly that all objects of consciousness appeared on an internal viewing screen, i.e., inside me. This view opened a new perspective or paradigm of self and world that contradicted the paradigm I had been operating with for twenty-five years, i.e., that the undefined "me" was inside and any objects in the view were outside me. I found that my mind could flip back and forth between these two contradictory paradigms or views and not be able to distinguish one as truer than the other.

The contradictory opposition of self being inside and things outside or vice versa had been oscillating back and forth in my mind for seven months when I went on a solitary retreat near Erie, PA in May 2004. During the retreat, Harding's tests for immortality (in his *Little Book of Life and Death*) brought my attention repeatedly back to looking at what I was looking out from. Those occurrences gradually brought me to the final faulty belief about the self, and then that was burned out by the truth of self-awareness.

Douglas provided the catalyst that completed my journey. Along with many others who received his beneficence, as long as memory lasts I'll be inexpressibly grateful for a wonderful friend.[17]

~ Art

---

[17] From the February 2007 "TAT Forum, "www.tatfoundation.org/forum2007-02.htm

Feedback to Art

It was a Saturday mini-retreat in the spring of 2000 in Pittsburgh. The topic of the meeting was "What is your true nature"?

Found this feedback that I had written for Art in my self-inquiry journal. Interesting to notice how we are not very different. Our underlying fears and desires, how we define ourselves, are almost the same. There is nothing special about our individual stories. You are born, you suffer and you die if you don't find your True Nature. Precious opportunity goes to waste.

Art: Self-deluded. You have no faith in yourself. Hopelessness seems like your chief feature. You think you don't have the answers and the ones you get, you don't trust.

What does True-Nature mean to you?
Where is yourSelf?
I know you have a strange love/hate relationship with yourself. You don't want to look deeper within to find the answers. That is why you think other people's findings will provide you with answers.
Why are you so hesitant to look within? Do you think that God is everywhere except in you? How long will you kid yourself?
Do you see your biggest obstacle?
What is the underlying belief about your lack of faith in 'you'?
Who lacks this faith/trust in Self/You?

~ Anima

Wakil's Dream

In 2007, Lieutenant Colonel Christopher Kolenda was commanding a Forward Operating Base in northern Kunar province of Afghanistan, a main conduit for moving Taliban and Al Qaeda weapons and fighters into Afghanistan from Pakistan. He emailed Greg Mortenson[18] about his conviction that "education will make the difference whether the next generation [of Afghanis] grows up to be educated patriots or illiterate fighters" and asking for help in the development of schools in his district.

Greg was hesitant to have his foundation linked in the Afghanis' minds to any military operations, but several email exchanges with Kolenda started eroding his reluctance to help. And finally his admiration for what the commander stood for and was trying to accomplish won him over.

But he needed to find someone who could pull it off. And that somebody who came to mind was an Afghani named Wakil he'd met five years earlier, who had lived in a Pakistani refugee camp from age 7 until he was nearly 23, shortly before Greg met him managing a guest house in Kabul. He phoned Wakil to ask him if he thought he could safely make a week-long scouting trip to the village across the river from the forward operating base where Kolenda wanted to build the first school.

Wakil drove to Jalalabad, where he met a friend who had relatives in Kunar. They spent the night in an inn there, and several other guests told them chilling reports of their time in Kunar. Wakil had a wife, six children, a mother and other relatives dependent on him, so he was debating with himself about continuing on to Kunar or returning home.

---

18   See "Stumbling into Love" in Chapter 7 of this book.

In the night he had a dream, where he was typing at a keyboard in front of a computer screen. Whenever he pressed the Enter key, the screen turned bright green; whenever he pressed the Backspace key, it turned brown. Back and forth: green then brown.

The following morning after breakfast he said to his friend that it was time to go. His friend, who was aware of his concern, said you mean go back to Kabul? Wakil told him no, to Kunar. And then he described his dream and what he was convinced it meant: If we don't go forward and help the people build their school, the whole area will become dry and brown. And he concluded that he couldn't ignore a dream that revealed what Allah wanted him to do.

~ Art

Struggling Blindly

Struggling blindly
in the fog of beliefs,
you grasp first one then another
in the quest for security.

What you seek lies between and behind these beliefs.
I am the respectful doubt,
the solvent that detaches beliefs.

Believe in Me.

~ Art

What Seekers Can Learn from Sikhism: The Path of Service

Last winter I got to visit the Golden Temple in Amritsar. It is a chief Gurudwara[19] of Sikhs. To see the lights and to participate in the last service of the day, we decided to go at night. What really struck me about the whole environment was the volunteers. There were lots of people just busy cleaning, mopping, serving prasad[20] in the middle of the night. Though it was really cold, everyone was barefoot. You don't wear shoes inside religious places in India. My feet were freezing on the cold marble floor, and so I could imagine the discomfort of the volunteers as well. While doing their chores everyone was constantly chanting 'Waheguru' which literally means "wondrous guru"; it also can mean "guru who fills my heart with joyous wonder." God, Absolute, is also referred to as Guru in the Sikh religion.

Sewa[21] as a path towards Truth is emphasized in Sikhism. A Sikh, which means a learner, disciple, or seeker of truth while living the life of a householder, strives to remain connected to the Divine in his heart. He views his daily life as an opportunity to serve the Guru who is in all. Though spiritual practices, selfless service, self-discipline, and right lifestyle are seen as progression towards your goal of Liberation, it is only through continual devotion and focus on the Divine that you attain Liberation. While you live in the

---

19 Temple, House of worship
20 Literally, a gracious gift
21 Service

world, your mind is attuned to God which is One. 'Tu Hee' meaning 'Only You' lies at the core of bhakti.[22]

Guru Arjan Dev, the fifth Sikh guru, when he was being tortured and executed by Jahangir, the Mughal emperor, kept saying, "All is happening, O Waheguru, according to Thy Will. Thy Will is ever sweet to me."

Guru Har Gobind, the sixth guru, wore two swords, miri and piri, representing temporal power and spiritual power. He told his followers: "In the Guru's house, spiritual and mundane powers shall be combined. My rosary shall be the sword-belt, and on my turban I shall wear a Kalgi (ornament for the turban)."

Though Sikhism came about during the time of Mughal invasion and the Sikhs fought against tyranny, it is essentially a bhakti path. Ego is effaced by surrendering to the Guru, without whose guidance there can be no liberation. *Guru Granth Sahib* is the formless Guru for Sikhs. This is the sacred text of Sikhism, considered as the eleventh and final guru, the repository of God's revelation to humankind.

Sikhism shows a seeker of Truth how to establish a firm relationship with the Divine. Sewa, selfless service without any expectation of reward or personal gain, takes the focus off from the self. You serve with the attitude that the whole world emerged from one Essence. Serving others is serving the Guru. Sewa strengthens the love in your heart for One and All, where it becomes simply an expression of Love.

~ Anima

---

22 Devotion to God

Strategy

I know my Achilles heel is trying to understand everything intellectually (I also enjoy this very much :), but I really have no clue how to proceed in terms of meditation. So, if you have strats, shoot. Otherwise, I'll just "do nothing," however that plays out.

I've been reviewing my journals, which date from 1977 (imagine what it was like before you were born :-) for a book I'm working on. Just came across something this morning from March 1987, where I'd noted a comment in Richard Rose's *Direct-Mind Experience* from the transcript of a Kent State University radio interview: "If you don't have trouble, you're not going to think."

I had plenty of trouble, like you, and of course I tried to accommodate myself to it. If we're successful doing so, or if the trouble is lifted, we can return to a more comfortable state of hypnosis. Fortunately—in retrospect—the trouble never lifted from me, and I was never able to accommodate myself to it.

The type of thinking that Rose was referring to was "productive" thinking. He also used that term to describe the type of meditation he recommended. Nothing fancy, and nothing that can be reduced to a formula. It begins with the intuition that the solution to our misery is to realize what we truly are. What we're looking for can only be found within... and not just by looking within but by going within.

Rose tried to provide some practical pointers about going within in his *Meditation* booklet and also in *Psychology of the Observer*. I attempted to put his recommendations into practice over a 25-year period, and by the end of that period

I didn't think I had any better understanding of what "going within" meant that when I started. But then something happened & I found myself within... found myself.

Here's what I'd say about strategy. These are just opinions I'm trying to communicate, not something I'm trying to sell or get you to agree with:

1. Feel the deepest want (i.e., the feeling that something's lacking or missing) that you can feel.
2. Feeling that feeling generates commitment. After all, who doesn't want what they really want. There's no real contest then with lesser wants—we won't want them to interfere with satisfying our deepest want.
3. The commitment is naturally for as long as it takes, our entire lifetime if necessary, with no guarantee of success. That's also the way to live a life with no final regret.

One of the fellows in an email confrontation group asked me this recently:

> *When you talk about meditation, I think you underline that it has to be confrontational. After changing the focus of the meditation I practice, I checked your site to remember what you said about the topic. I found that you included a quote by Ramana [Maharshi] where he talks about japa, mantra repetition, to lead us to the Self. That was unexpected. Would you say that mantra repeating with devotion is an effective path?*

My response to him:

> I forget what all's on the website & am continually surprised at what I find there when somebody asks a

question that sets me to looking for the context. This quote by Nisargadatta on that same page[23] is another example of unexpected advice:

> Don't put in special efforts to witness, just be in a relaxed condition. You are studying your mind movements at mind level... You are practicing witnessing, you are not being the witness. There is no special effort to be made; it just takes place. About concentration: it is something like running around trying to take a photograph of the government of Bombay. Can you take a photograph of the government?... Why do you follow these exercises? Give them up. Just be relaxed in your natural state; that is the highest state. The lower state is concentration and meditation.

Ramana, in his talk about japa, appears to be describing something he had experienced... perhaps it was what preceded his daily samadhi periods in adult life. I'd say the best mantra or japa would be reminding oneself of what one really wants... feeling the feeling of one's deepest longing. The mind eventually falls in love with that which it desires... "Truth" was how it felt to me that I longed for... and calling for the Love is a devotional path. The question of what we are, or the problem of what we believe ourselves to be, is never far from the surface of the mind. If we encourage that natural quest of the mind for satisfaction, that is the core of a self-inquiry practice, and if we also call out to that which we love, that is the core of a devotional practice. I doubt if either one by itself would be as effective.

~ Art

---
23 selfdiscoveryportal.com/medexp.htm

I Don't Get It

What's the point of the game and sleeping in life? I'm half way home... how do I get all the way there?

I'm a tiny projection of myself (most likely an infinitely small projection within projections)... I'm constantly moving towards the centre from where I came... and one day I'll be united with the ONE and only Self... but why this game? Why all this heaven and hell? I'm still obviously not receiving all the signals. How can I do that?

The "why?" questions take our focus off the important question, M. We discover who or what we really are first—then we can focus on the whys and wherefores if they still appear relevant. Those questions are based on hearsay. We don't discover what we are by trying to understand hearsay, no matter how right it sounds. As for not receiving all the signals:

- It takes time for the mind to admit the truth of what it sees.
- When the mind has eliminated the make-believe it's holding onto, the Self irradiates the mind with its effulgence.
- You will then be able to say: "I can see him, but Mustafa can't see Me."
- There's no formula that will take the mind-self there.
- The teacher can help dispel illusion. Life is the great teacher.

~ Art

Time Capsule

It was the summer of 2003. There were about 6 of us for a PSI (Philosophical Self-Inquiry) retreat at the Richard Rose farm. The addition at the back of the farmhouse for TAT meetings was not very big, but surprisingly it could accommodate quite a few people when there was a need. The room had a large round wooden table, with rustic wooden chairs. Way back then, the largest gathering that I was a part of, was about 24 people. Everybody would happily fit in that room without complaining. There were rapport sittings, confrontations, discussions, presentations. All sorts of ways and means employed with the sole aim of finding Truth. I found that there was, and still is, a deep sense of camaraderie amongst TAT members. Love and gratitude for Mr. Rose become evident as soon as anyone starts sharing their stories about him and life on the farm.

The early 2000s were when TAT was going through a lean period. Mr. Rose was already in a nursing home with an advanced stage of Alzheimer's. Most of the people who lived on the farm had left. I was probably the newest, FOB,[24] member of TAT. The ruralness of the Rose farm somehow reminded me of the village and the farm back in India where I grew up: hills, tall trees, bushes, unpaved road, outhouse, wooden stoves, and temple bells ringing in the distance.

However, cicadas and their constant drone-like mating call described as "cacophonous whining like a field of out-of-tune car radios" was a completely new experience for me. I can still feel the cool summer breeze and hear the constant loud sound of cicadas. (On a side note, these insects go

---

24 Fresh off the boat.

underground for 13 to 17 years. And guess what? They are seen this year, in 2020, since last seen in 2003.)

Before I go on tangents and start with some other story, I should finish telling you about this particular evening session. Towards the end of the retreat, Art came up with this idea of creating a time capsule, with all of us writing about what we hope for TAT and what we hope for ourselves in the future. Art never fails to surprise me with the genius ideas that he thinks up for sessions. More to my amazement, after all these years he had this time capsule saved somewhere. An empty tennis ball holder tube was what served as the time capsule. It was interesting to get a peek into my own mind and what I was thinking on that particular Saturday evening on July 05th, 2003 at 7 pm.

TAT: I hope TAT would continue to grow and help to support other seekers. There would be more TAT members with their questions answered helping other fellow seekers by sharing their experience.

Me: Total acceptance of my little universe the way it is without a desire to change the smallest thing. Will know what is Permanent and Real. My heart would be totally at peace experiencing complete Freedom. I hope for Realization of the Self in the future.

~ Anima

4

Self-Inquiry

First Glimpse of Home

When we first fall in love with someone or something other than ourselves, we get our first adult glimpse of what the heart longs for. The clue that we experience is that our self is momentarily off the stage rather than in the spotlight.

If we persist in our search for Truth or Reality or Self, we reach a point where it becomes intuitively obvious that the self we believe ourselves to be is what's in the way. By then the momentum of our search keeps us going despite realizing that there's nothing in it for us. This is deflating to the sense of self, the individuality sense, but if we're fortunate, we've experienced the great relief that occurs when the self is out of the picture, and that memory helps us persevere.

The ego death that accompanies Self-realization doesn't leave us either as unfeeling zombies or as blissful dolts. The mental machinery still functions—now without the impedance that ego-identification creates.

~ Art

Let Death Be Your Teacher

This is a story of a dialogue between a teenage boy, Nachiketa, and Yama.[25] It comes from the Katha Upanishad.[26] It is a highly dramatic confrontational dialogue between the ideal teacher, death, and an ideal student, who refuses everything except for Self-knowledge.

Nachiketa's father, the sage *Vājashravas*, decided to perform a big Yajna[27] to please the gods and to improve his chances in the next life. It was a big occasion. There were lots of rishis attending, mantras were chanted, offerings made to the fire, and there was a big feast. This Yagna entailed giving away all your worldly possessions. Cows were considered valuable and prized possessions in those times. Hence *Vājashravas* decided to donate his cows to the Brahmins.

Nachiketa noticed that his father was only giving away old and disabled cows. These cows were no longer capable of bearing calves or giving milk. The boy saw through his father's worldly cleverness. To dissuade his father from accumulating bad karma, he asked him in a loud whisper to whom will he donate him since *Vājashravas* was supposed to give away all his possessions. His father ignored Nachiketa initially but when he insisted, *Vājashravas* got angry and said that he would give him to death, to Yama. As the moment of

---

25 Lord of Death.
26 The Upanishads constitute the end part of the Vedic Sanskrit text. There are 108 Upanishads, having the central theme of the deathless Self and the way to Its realization. The Katha Upanishad (Kaṭhopaniṣad) is one of the popular ones. It starts with the story of Nachiketa and Yama, the lord of death.
27 A Yajna or Yagna is a ritual sacrifice, done in front of a sacred fire, with a specific objective.

anger passed, *Vājashravas* regretted what he said. But it was too late. Nachiketa reminded him that he couldn't go back on his word, especially when it came to making sacrifices for the Yagna.

The story goes that Yama was not home when Nachiketa reached his abode. Nachiketa waited outside Yama's home for three days before Yama returned. Seeing a Brahmin boy waiting for him without food, water, or sleep, Yama felt bad. Thus he granted him three wishes for his three days of waiting. The first wish Nachiketa asked for was that his father should not remain angry with him.

Yama granted him this wish. The second wish was to learn the proper way to perform a secret fire sacrifice that leads one to heaven. Yama taught Nachiketa the correct procedure, giving him all the instructions. Yama was so pleased with Nachiketa that he even named this particular Yagna after his new student.

The third wish that Nachiketa asked for was to know if something exists after death. He wanted all his doubts about life and death to be dispelled. Yama was a little taken aback. He tried to dissuade Nachiketa by telling him that the secret of death was hard to know even for gods. He told Nachiketa to ask for something else. Anything. Yama offered him a long, pleasurable life with an abundance of whatever Nachiketa could desire.

Being a stubborn teenager and aware of impending death, Nachiketa asked what pleasure can be more than fleeting for a mortal. He pointed out that pleasures just drain vital energy. Nachiketa questioned how one who is subject to old age and death can be made happy with wealth. What could you desire when you see the face of death getting closer? How can you live a life when you do not know what life is? Moreover, without knowing who is this that is living, everything becomes meaningless. The only thing that

Self-Inquiry

Nachiketa wanted was for Yama to dispel his doubts about death and to know what, if anything, does not decay and does not change. Is there anything that remains when the body dies?

Yama finally had to give in. Nachiketa learned from the Lord of death the path to Self-Realization. Yama, being the practical teacher, teaches his student how to find the Truth, the Source of all. He teaches him to discriminate between *shreya* (better/good) which moves us closer to our goal, perennial joy; and *preya* (merely pleasant), passing pleasure. Yama instructs Nachiketa to choose his actions wisely.

He also explains to him how to live a life that is aligned with your core desire. Yama explains that the seeker, the body-mind, is like a chariot and a charioteer. Desires and fears are what give direction to how life unfolds. Body is the chariot, the vehicle. It is only meant to serve its driver. The senses are like horses, if you do not control them by putting blinds on the sides, they will run in all directions; but when you direct them wisely, they will take you to your destination swiftly. Mind is the rein that controls the horses. With the right amount of tension, it directs the horses, how fast and in the right direction to go. The charioteer is the intellect that decides what is the purpose of this life and how to fulfill that purpose. It is the intellect that directs the mind. And yet intellect cannot reveal the Self, which is beyond duality. It cannot come through logic and scholarship but from close association with a realized teacher. Yama gives Nachiketa knowledge of eternal Self.

The question "Who Am I?" becomes most urgent and serious only in the face of death. This grim awareness of death puts a question mark to all aspects of our life. Let death be your teacher.

~ Anima

Opening Your Heart

I feel like I get more out of meditation if I'm in a "softer" state of mind, similar to the state of mind you noticed me in (and pointed out) during the last day [of a week-long retreat]. Knowing what you know of me, what can I do to get into this state of mind more often, especially before meditation? It seems like a vulnerable state I want to avoid at most times, but there are times I'm willing to get into it if it means I'll make progress.

I think you've hit the nail on the head: vulnerability... and specifically the belief that we're vulnerable to (able to be wounded by) feelings. The sensitive intellect is largely a response to emotional vulnerability, a defense mechanism to try to ward off feelings that threaten to overwhelm the ego. Why haven't you jumped into self-definition, which intellectually you see as the only hope of salvation? Could it be fear by the ego, with its rational defense structure, of being overwhelmed? Overwhelmed by what? Certainly not by thought... but by feeling, by the irrational?

"We try to be so rock-ribbed, we poor mortals!" as Alfred Pulyan[28] wrote to Richard Rose. What is the nature of your prayer before meditating? Is it rational or irrational? Do you lay your heart open to the Lord, to your Inner Self? Do you feel the pain of humanity as it calls out for comfort (literally, strength through unison)? Is this what you're trying to get from relationships? It's a great burden to project on another human being.

Softening requires relaxation, like opening the fist. Meditating to become conscious of what we really are

---
28 See http://selfdiscoveryportal.com/Pulyan.htm/.

requires acknowledging our existential angst, feeling the pain of existence. When it becomes intuitively obvious to us that whatever created us (the Creative Principal is a good, neutral phrase used by Hubert Benoit in *The Supreme Doctrine*) hasn't abandoned us but is, in fact, the inner self that we're searching for, then we can honestly open ourselves to ask the inner self for help.

Of course we first have to get to the point where we admit the need for help. Once that occurs, then our pre-meditation softening or opening up proceeds along the lines of allowing ourselves to feel the existential angst and then feeling our connection to the inner source or self.

~ Art

Rapport

Would you like to feel love?
Raise the portcullis,
drop the drawbridge.
Love is within,
but we stay out.
Begin with fresh eyes:
see your friend for the first time.
The door is open.
At the center
you and the friend
are not two.

~ Art

When Confrontation Works

Confronting someone's beliefs, by helping them question those beliefs—with the goal of gaining some detachment from the fear- and pride-egos that masquerade as the self—is a tricky proposition. Art admits that the way he goes about it is by trial and error (or persistent stumbling, as he describes his own path toward self-definition). When it's effective, the recipient sometimes recognizes it, as in the following comments by a participant in an email confrontation and accountability group:

I've been feeling a subtle relinquishing or softening since the TAT weekend. I came back and things at work and with relationships and all the rest don't seem like the massive problems they were. I guess I feel a little more sober, all told.

During the confrontation session at the intensive, Art honed in on the fact that my desires shift frequently. Some desires can be seen through in advance, and others must be followed in order to know if in fact that is what I really want. The basic idea was to just be honest with whatever it is that I really want, and not keep playing a game of charades with the universe. I never before felt that it was okay to look at what I really want without the voice of judgment, particularly the voice that says "You've got to do the 'spiritual thing' first." The message I got was not, "You can get off the hook," but "Just be honest with what your heart really desires." It was the same message that Rumi gets at here:

> Let yourself be silently drawn
> by the strange pull of what you really love.
> It will not lead you astray.

The rapport that followed the confrontation left an indelible fingerprint on consciousness, like a genuine whisper of the Absolute, that lingered for several days.

~ Anima (italicized paragraphs are from a participant in an email confrontation group)

Salvation

I know that both career and loved ones won't be the permanent answer that will end my angst. To be honest, I don't believe that the end to suffering is attainable for me. So I'm settling down for less, holding on to what I think is the next best thing, no matter how impermanent and insufficient.

Especially this past week I have not been setting aside time to be alone and do nothing. I opted for spending time with my close friend in his temporary visit. I don't believe that any resolution of my biggest fear can be reached in solitary reflections. I am tired of locking myself up and working alone. I need a savior.

The savior you're looking for is omnipresent. It's the trigger that opens "the mind" (i.e., the movie that you're watching) so that it no longer grasps onto the faulty belief of being a separate sentient being. The experience of salvation is the experience of falling in love. The most frequent occurrence is falling in love with a child (you could ask your mother about that); the next most frequent may be falling in love with an idealized person, like Jesus or Muhammad. Those are partial, temporary openings, and each one is accompanied by a disillusionment. That's for the emotional mind. For the intellectual mind, disillusionment is the predominant aspect of progress, accompanied by a feeling (love) that the mind may not consciously feel. Don't be afraid to love.

~ Art

Silence

Silence
covered with noisy thoughts
And roaring waves
Is not quietness.
Is not dead
Or death

Is not nothingness
No-thingness maybe

Silence
Alive and Pulsating
Current
Underlying
All around
Everywhere

You can feel it
In your cells
Hair follicles
Flowing out of you
Immersing you

Try tuning into it

~ Anima

I Believe That....

My *self definition is created through relationships.*

It's true that definition in the mind-realm requires comparison. But self-comparisons such as "I'm my mother's daughter," or "I'm a better writer than her," etc., define body origins, body products, and so on. So they're really saying: "I am this body, and here are some characteristics of this body in relation to or comparison with other bodies.

Are you the body? The body-mind?

Going within, or climbing Jacob's ladder, requires comparison with the opposite. How would you define yourself in terms of what you're not?

❧

I think.

What exactly does "I think" mean to you: Do you create thoughts? Decide what thoughts to have before you experience them? An experiment: If you watch closely, what do you observe happening if you try to think only thoughts of art history for 10 minutes?

I experimented with your exercise this week, and the results have been the same so far: When I observed, at first there were usually no thoughts. Then there were intruder-thoughts appear (those random ones which seem to come out of nowhere and are not my creations). Then I remembered I was supposed to think art history thoughts, so there were words such as "art history," "painting," "*impressionism,*" the name of my professors, and really silly unconnected combinations of words. But I still believe I produced those art history thoughts because I have an explanation (even when it sounds ridiculous): I've become so good at producing thoughts that it feels as if I just waved my magic wand and poof! thoughts appear. Easy.

If *you* are making thoughts appear, then you should be able to pick out a single thought that has appeared and 1) see when you decided to produce that thought, 2) see the mechanism by which you preselected that particular thought and the exact wording of it, and 3) see the mental apparatus (finger, elbow, etc.) *you* used to control the mechanism. Can you find an example?

~ Art

Facing Fear & Depression

In his biographical book *A Journey: My Political Life*, Tony Blair described the weekly Prime Minister's Questions (PMQs) that were perhaps the most horrific part of his job for ten years as Britain's PM. They're an institution of the British Parliament where the opposition basically tries to humiliate the PM. He wrote in 2010, years after his terms in office (1997-2007):

> Even today, wherever I am in the world, I feel a cold chill at 11:57 a.m. on Wednesdays, a sort of prickle on the back of my neck, the thump of the heart. That was the moment I used to be taken from the prime minister's room in the House of Commons through to the Chamber itself. I used to call it the walk from the cell to the place of execution.

How did he deal with it?

> I got braver. I realised that in the end I had to confront the demons. It was no use praying more the night before, wearing the right shoes (I wore the same pair of Church's brogues every PMQs for ten years) or just hoping I would get by. I decided to analyse it, and try to work out how to do it to the best of my ability.
>
> I remember as a schoolboy doing boxing, which was compulsory. I loathed it; I could never see the point of it nor understand its appeal. In the first fights, I was scared. I didn't want to hit my opponent. I didn't want him to hit me. I just wanted the thing over with. After a time, though, I chose to box properly, to stand my ground and fight. I did it with fear, but also with

determination. Either do it properly or refuse to do it at all—that's also fine—but don't do it like a wuss. I didn't like boxing any better, but I respected myself more.

Gradually, I evolved a pattern of working for PMQs. It all started with a determination to be braver, to stand my ground and fight, consciously. Fear as a stimulus, in proper proportion, can keep you on your toes. Fear that tumbles into panic is all bad. In the early days, I wouldn't sleep well the night before or eat at all in the morning. The first thing I realised was the importance of being in the right physical as well as mental condition, so I changed my routine. I took a melatonin pill the night before so I got at least six hours' sleep. I made sure I had a proper breakfast, and just before the ordeal began, I would eat a banana to give myself energy It seems daft, but I was finding that my energy levels, and thus my mental agility, were dropping after ten minutes. It really made a difference. At 12:28 I was still alive to the risks and up to repelling the assault.

Elizabeth Gilbert, author of *Eat, Love, Pray* (and subject of the 2010 film of that title starring Julia Roberts), wrote in *Committed: A Skeptic Makes Peace with Marriage:*

> Between my romantic entanglements and my professional obsessions [she wrote predominantly for and about men], I was so absorbed by the subject of maleness that I never spent any time whatsoever contemplating the subject of femaleness. I certainly never spent any time contemplating my *own* femaleness. For that reason, as well as a general indifference toward my own well-being, I never became very familiar to myself. So when a massive wave of depression finally struck me down around the age of thirty I had no way of understanding or articulating what was happening to me. My body fell apart first, then my marriage, and then—for a terrible and frightening interval—my mind.

Self-Inquiry

Masculine flint offered no solace in this situation; the only way out of the emotional tangle was to feel my way through it. Divorced, heartbroken, and lonely, I left everything behind and took off for a year of travel and introspection, intent on scrutinizing myself as closely as I'd once studied the elusive American cowboy.

Panics and depression are emotional tangles. These accounts of how Blair and Gilbert faced their internal demons are instructive of a success formula for doing the same. The mind first has to get to the point of being tired or fed up with its state or with a particular reaction pattern. When that occurs, its decision-making apparatus reacts with determination to contemplate, question, and overcome the debilitating condition. Blair's reaction focused on analysis, Gilbert's on feeling her way through it. Both are based on looking at the mind's operation, including the desire and fear factors moving it, rather than looking away. It's a struggle… but one that pays off when we persevere.

~ Art

Nuts and Bolts

The George Observatory in Houston is my favorite place to visit on a clear summer evening. There are these huge telescopes on the roof of the building.

> Depending on the time of the month and the season of the year, visitors are able to observe a variety of phenomena, such as Saturn's rings, cloud belts on Jupiter, a partial or total eclipse of the Moon, a bright meteor or fireball that lights up the ground, the Milky Way, or a close pairing of two planets. Stargazers can look at the night sky through George Observatory's telescopes, far away from the light pollution of the big city.[29]

To get a clear view of the moon or any other object in deep space, you have to adjust the telescope. The object is there. There is a viewer who is keen to see the object. And then there is an apparatus required that makes it possible for the viewer to see the object clearly. Just like a telescope needs to be adjusted to see the celestial objects, there are certain tendencies of the mind that can be aligned to find Truth. Preparation of the mind for the accident to happen.

In response to Arjuna's question[30] to "What is gyana?", Krishna enumerates twenty qualities of the mind that he calls gyana[31] or knowledge. These are attitudes of the mind which come naturally as the seeker becomes serious towards his goal of finding Truth. Any value, unless it is internalized

---

[29] The George Observatory website (https://www.hmns.org/george-observatory/).
[30] In the *Bhagavad Gita*.
[31] Sometimes spelled *jnana*.

and has become a natural aspect of a seeker, is simply empty words.

To me, it is Krishna teaching Arjuna to hold his head right, such that Truth, Braham[32] is realized by this warrior. These are Inner Values assimilated for gaining Self-Knowledge. If Krishna took time to teach these to Arjuna, as he must have known what would be helpful to find Truth, I think it merits serious consideration from any seeker. Here are the values that help a seeker in preparing a receptive and objective state of mind for Truth:

Absence of conceit: When a person has seen and accepted his limitations and qualifications. Not to confuse self-respectfulness with self-conceit though. There is no more demand for respect or applause from others for your achievement. The rosebush does not need appreciation but blooms because that is its nature. When inflated ego and pride is observed for what it is, the mind becomes emptied of conceit.

Absence of pretense: Pretense manifesting as self-glorification. The pretense may or may not be just external for the world but with ourselves. Needing to portray 'me' as a little better than what I am, or condemning myself for what I see as my limitations. Conceit, pretense, hypocrisy arises out of a deep rejection of the relative self. Such a state of mind is unable to accept relative truth as it is engaged in hiding and protecting its false image. It hides behind complexities.

---

[32] Also written as Brahman; the ultimate reality underlying all phenomena.

❧

Not hurting: Inherent in the desire of man to live free of pain. "Do unto others as you have them do unto you," the Bible says. Not wanting to cause pain or harm to the other comes from my inner desire to live in harmony and peace with myself. Ahimsa[33] cannot be just in deeds or actions but also in words and thoughts.

❧

Glad acceptance, which is mostly understood as peace with underlying connotations of resigned forbearance. The attitude of Kshanti,[34] as explained by Swami Dayananda Saraswati,[35] is "I cheerfully, calmly accept that behavior and those situations, which I cannot change. I give up the expectations or demands that the other person or situation should change in order to conform to what would be pleasing to me. I happily accept and accommodate situations and people." This requires an understanding of human nature which is directly proportional to how well you understand your own self.

---

33 Respect for all living things and avoidance of violence toward others.
34 Patience, forbearance and forgiveness.
35 Vedantic teacher and founder of Arsha Vidya Gurukulam.

❧

Straightness or Rectitude: Alignment of thoughts, words and actions based on one's ethical standards. When my actions are not true to my words, and my words are not true to my thoughts, it creates dissonance, a splintered mind. You become unreliable to yourself.

❧

Service and surrender to the teacher: Reflects a state of mind for a student characterized by a willingness to surrender personal ego, devotion and respect towards the teacher coming from the heart. This is essential if a student desires to gain knowledge. Even when the teacher has no need for the student's devotion and surrender or any other service.

❧

Inner and outer purity: Maintaining the daily discipline of external hygiene is not even a question to live a clean, healthy life. But what about mental hygiene? The mind gets cluttered and unclean as well. Maintaining mental hygiene, where it is free of daily irritations and resentments or driven by the roller coaster of emotions, cannot be undermined for a seeker. Introspection and self-observation help in breaking the reactive patterns of mind, making it alert to its own conditioning.

Firmness, Constancy, Steadfastness, Perseverance: We all start with the best intentions to apply the best effort towards our goal, but as the initial enthusiasm wanes, we start looking for excuses to give up. Self-knowledge, unlike knowledge of some discipline, is a total knowledge—the total content of all knowledge. All other goals get resolved with the goal of finding self-knowledge. Lack of perseverance will lead to giving in to distractions and laziness and thus failure to achieve your goal.

Mastery over mind: Mind is the colorful kaleidoscope of interesting thoughts that come and go. Rarely still, busy in reverie, whimsical by nature. Do I, the thinker, have any control over what it does? Is it in alignment with my life purpose? It does get shaped by my ways of thinking. The content of thought changes the way the brain, the apparatus, gets shaped. Seekers can only aim for relative mastery of the mind, which would be of thoughts based on impulsive instincts; of mechanical, prior conditioning; deliberation comes with evaluating processes and functions of the mind. When you become deliberate in your thinking, you have reached relative mastery. The aligning of your inner values with the universal values only comes with Self-Knowledge. Now you have become a Master of the Universe.

Dispassion towards sense objects, or absence of a compelling drive for worldly pleasures and possessions. Does this mean suppression of your wants and desires? No, dispassion is a state of mind that comes from a total objectivity towards worldly objects. Dispassion is not suppression of desire but absence of compelling desires. It comes from seeing what my relationships are to these objects that I am hankering for. Lasting fulfillment, the completeness that I really want, cannot come from any amount of wealth or from even the most pleasurable objects. Objects do serve a purpose, but they are not to be mistaken for curing your inner dis-ease.

Absence of self-importance: Freedom from an individualized 'I-sense', egotism. When I take credit for what happens in life, good or bad… 'I do', 'I own', 'I enjoy'. Pride in being the doer, a special and unique individual, keeps you stuck in your ignorance. Ego is nothing else but an uninvestigated belief in what we think we are. Humility is a natural state of a seeker who understands the world, including himself, the way it is. Pride or self-condemnation disappears with simple understanding and acceptance of life and you in it. Self-condemnation, inferiority, or the need to compare are nothing else but ego expressing itself. Life experiences are seen as opportunities to discover your true nature without pride or egotism.

Reflections on the limitations of birth, death, old age, sickness and pain: What is born will die. When death comes, it is not in your control. The nature of life is that there is no predictability; man suffers from external, internal and existential ailments. No one can escape sickness and old age. It is just a matter of time before you start noticing the aging body. Krishna is suggesting to Arjuna that by reflecting on these life conditions, you maintain perspective on what is important, the purpose of your life.

Absence of sense of ownership: When you feel you own something, your relationship to it changes. Your desire to 'hold fast' to your possessions, house, property. Your clinging attachment to what you think you own does not allow your mind to have space for any other thought. Simply asking "what really is mine" breaks this hypnotic attachment and helps see my relationship to things objectively.

Absence of obsession with son, wife, house and so on: Intense attachment or affection towards people who are very important and dear to us. What underlies this obsessive love is the inner lack we feel. We try to fill it with obsessive love towards the other. It does not mean to abandon your family or stop loving them, but caring and showing affection with dispassion.

Constant equanimity towards desirable and undesirable results: Accepting results as they come, without any personal preference, objectively. A mind unshaken by emotional reactions. A mind that can calmly decide what needs to be done and can execute the action. A mind that can maintain equilibrium regardless of the results, not swinging between elation or depression.

Unswerving devotion to Me characterized by non-separateness from Me: When you know that the source of everything is only One, the mind then becomes relatively poised, not muddled by its projections. Graceful acceptance of the result is prasada (blessing from God). There is no regret, no failure, no elation or depression but freedom from all expectations and reactions.

Preferences for a secluded place: The tendency of the mind is to stay engaged in some activity, to not have to look at itself. This is to escape that underlying feeling of incompletion. A mind that becomes quiet prefers solitude and loves to be with itself. A simple, quiet, contemplative mind is ready for clear knowledge of itself.

Absence of craving for social interactions: Krishna is pointing out the value that means a lack of craving for company. This does not mean hating or avoiding people but not using busyness with other humans to escape from our inner discomfort with being with ourselves.

Understanding the ultimate validity of Self-knowledge: Keeping in view the purpose of the knowledge of truth. Why should you look for Self-knowledge? Why should it be your primary goal in life? What is gained by Self-knowledge? It does not help in fulfilling your worldly duties, or in getting objects of pleasure or security. It does lead to moksha, liberation from the human sense of limitation, of incompleteness. Freedom from desire itself. The mature mind seeks Truth, knowledge of Self, for the sake of knowing. For the love for Truth.

Commitment to Self-knowledge: Using listening, reflection and contemplation, the seeker pursues Self-knowledge till he gets the truth of oneself... "I Am That".

~ Anima

Nostalgia

In togetherness and silence...
On my evening walk with Toby[36]
I noticed
the day ready to meet the night, the orangy dusk
air filled with smell of the earthy musk.
The reddish blue sky
patterned with rows of birds returning to their nests
Eagle's strong wings flying him to his place of rest.

Heart gets a bit heavy...
I can feel that familiar mood
descending
This little ache in my heart, is it longing?
triggered
by a simple melody of that sweet love song;
A memory of the warmth oozing from the burning coals
of the earthen fire pit.
Sound of the rain falling outside;
Lightning coming through the rumbling clouds.
Koel[37] cuckooing from the mango tree.
Bits and pieces of memories
from now and then
flow out of the crevices of my ancient mind
And cause that slight twinge in my rib cage

Most of the time...
this feeling, considered unnecessary

---
36   Anima's dog.
37   Cuckoo bird.

Always Right Behind You

gets ignored.
Preferred to be buried
deep down under
the business of living and catching up

Too bad, how sad,
you can't see
that this is your ticket
to get on the fastest train
that can take you Home
for Eternal Rest.

~ Anima

Turning Attention from Not-Self

What decides that awareness needs to "shine the light" on itself? If you're working from the level of the umpire, is it the umpire's mechanism of perceived duality that ultimately betrays itself? Is this why people seem to need their "hair on fire" (intense desire / earnestness / recognition of an intense problem) / experience frustration through the process to attain their goal?

When the goal of self-realization is not realized, is it this frustration/perceived negative experience unable to be resolved by the "umpire" (dual programmed thinking) that forces the umpire to look anteriorly for an opposite. (I understand the umpire is merely a metaphor, but I also understand this to be a system of working backwards... maybe I'm wrong.) Does this frustration force the view from perceived horizontal opposites on the bottom of the triangle to a movement of vertical opposites pushing it up to the next apex of the anterior triangle since it seems to be a mechanism of the umpire to identify self and not self (opposites)? Maybe I'm over thinking this in an unsophisticated way, and I guess [Richard Rose's "Jacob's Ladder"] is not a physical diagram but a relationship of each point to itself and to the true viewer. I ask as in my meditation technique... (identification of the "not me") I'm using the umpire..."this is X; this isn't X." If I weren't doing so, I wouldn't turn my attention away from the not-me, right?

Most of us never feel that our hair is on fire other than on rare occasions. Successful seeking for the truth is mostly what seems like a never-ending slog through thick mud and directionless swamps. I think it's more productive to look to see what's-what rather than try to twist ourselves into some other what-could-be.

Always Right Behind You

The desire to look anteriorly, to find where we came from—our source—is a curiosity to see our essential Self or a longing to go Home. The reason isn't too important. What's important, I believe, is the intuition picking up the feeling that what we're looking for is back along the ray of creation... back through the projector.

The taco-like reflexivity of the mind—it's ability to look back on itself, as if it were the inside of a taco shell—is merely the way it's structured. If it weren't for that, we wouldn't know that we're conscious and, I assume, couldn't become conscious of our essence. What Richard Rose termed the umpire is a decision-making program that's running all the time. The mind is more or less conscious of its operation depending on things such as hormonal tides and other emotional catalysts. The umpire's program appears to be the healthy functioning of the organism... and obviously it's not error-free code. But the basic algorithm is to always look for a solution to a problem in its opposite: too many calories => cut back on calories, too much booze => cut back on booze, too much drama => cut back on drama, and so on. The jump to an anterior position seems to be accidental... and there are only two such interior jumps, with the third being a jump beyond the mind.

Whenever the mind is conscious of an object (all objects being "not me" in the paradigm of self = the viewer, not-self = the view) there's always an implied subject... the difference being that the mind-self is never in the view. It always seems to be behind the head's view / within the heart. The feeling of self is always right behind us.

You love (identify with) "your" body. You love "your" thoughts, your story....

~ Art

And God Smiled

From Anima
Re. PA retreat
May 21, 2004

Hi Art,

Thanks for the poem.[38] It is sweet and made me smile. I have so many questions that I want to ask you. They are kind of silly though but i can't help these... :)

- is mind really the bridge that you need to cross over... what does it mean...
- was Art really never alive... what about this body suit we are wearing...
- does that inner eye turn away from this view and look back... is there an inner eye that can look at itself...
- **what is God... what does he/she feel like...**
- what does the small ego of Art do these days...
- do you think I'll lose this separate self some day...
- what is this no-thingness / every-thingness that people write about... what did you find...

I have more questions... :)... looking forward to your email. miss you...

---

38 See "I Am Always Right Behind You" in Chapter 8.

From Art
May 21, 2004
Dear friend,

(Art had a breakthrough, on a solitary retreat about 2 weeks earlier, after 26 years of conscious searching. He'd sent a report about the retreat to several friends and fellow seekers, including Anima.)

Glad to hear your reaction. Both K. P. and J. M. had the same reaction. In fact, J. said she grinned the whole time she read the isolation notes. That's probably the Joy in thee that's the same as in me and all god's little ones.

Here goes with responses to your questions. Don't worry too much about the words. I think the important thing is to pick up a feeling about what needs our attention next (in addition to the bambinos... :)

is mind really the bridge that you need to cross over... what does it mean...

- I think mind is what keeps us focused outward, identified with what we see outside ourself (creations of our Self).
- In my case, I didn't sense the mind stopping—it seemed able to continue on with its thinking without interfering with the observation process.
- But something seemingly has to break the hypnosis of the outward focus and set up a simultaneous (maybe not with some cases, where thinking stops) looking back into what we're looking from. The Harding exercises may do the trick in some cases.

Self-Inquiry

- What we're looking out of is Self-aware... which doesn't make any sense to the mind... and doesn't need our help... :)
- To really admit what we see when looking back at what we're looking out of—i.e., that It is Self-aware—doesn't happen until we simultaneously admit that whatever form of subtle observer we thought we were is not a separate "thing" aware of Self-awareness. My realization or admission or acceptance of that was translated back to the mind as "Art T. was never alive."

was Art really never alive... what about this body suit we are wearing...

- ha—just anticipated and answered the first part of this question... :)
- Art body-mind is a creation of the one-and-only real Self—an animated show being viewed by the Self in a seemingly complex way, since the AP body-mind, one of 6 billion similar creations also imbued with the conviction that it's alive, is seemingly also viewing the Art-story—although that's really the Self viewing the Art-story through the AP-animation. In other words, the stories are integrated. And the Animator is viewing the interaction of the animations. The difference is pointed out by Harding in that the Art-animation has no head when the Self is viewing the AP-story through it, but it does have a head when it's being viewed through the headless AP-animation. Get it?

does that inner eye turn away from this view and look back... is there an inner eye that can look at itself...

- There is only one Eye, one Observer, which apparently views pictures of "things" it has created for a reason that it doesn't seem to know. ("Why" only applies on the periphery, in the stories, where there is time, space, causation, etc.)
- In an intermediate stage, where we haven't yet admitted our non-existence as an individual something, it feels as if Art or AP has opened the proverbial third eye which is now looking back at what is at the core, at what Art or AP is looking out from—back along the ray of creation in Richard Rose's poetic phrasing.

what is God... what does he/she feel like...

- God smiled at this question... :)
- She/I must be female—she seems to have no idea why she's doing what she's doing...:)
- I think the mind only gets a narrow impression— perhaps mine being even narrower than many others'.
- So... imagine something with absolutely no features (a Terribly Plain Jane)... in fact so few features that it's not even a thing... an absolute No-thing... with no wristwatch or clock (it has to create galaxies with planets whirling around suns in order to tell what time it is)... with not a muscle to twitch nor a hair to get out of place... ain't never changed and never

Self-Inquiry

will... couldn't find a stitch of clothes to wear if it wanted to, since it has no boundaries... and so forth.
- And yet the damn funny thing is that its creations feel.

what is the small ego of Art doing these days...

- Have no fear—it's "alive" and kicking and less inhibited than ever. The anxiety it lived with for its entire self-conscious life seems to have disappeared.
- Everything's the same as it was... with one slight attitude adjustment...:)

do you think I'll lose this separate self some day...

- I'd say you're a good candidate.
- The truth is We already know Ourself, but we've managed to distract Ourself with the fascinating pictures we've created.
- The pictures aren't alive, but they're created to think so—and to think and feel all sorts of stuff—and to have a hidden longing or yearning to "remember" their Self through realizing that their self-awareness is really Self-awareness—that I and my Creator are not-two.
- The separate selves are creations with limited shelf-lives. One thing for sure is that their belief in separate existence will end—possibly before the animation itself reaches a complete halt.
- I don't think that we as Creator "know" how the story of Art or AP is going to turn out. We apparently want

to experience it in time, sort of like a mystery novel. Possibly there's an occasional "foreshadowing" (a device that novelists use to give a hint as to what's coming) or even a "sneak preview" (as when one of the animations has been created with a scene where it foresees something in its or another animation's "future" unfolding).

what is this no-thingness/every-thingness that people write about... what did you find...

- I saw—or the mind understood, as mental doubts were quelled seemingly by repeated seeing—in two stages that what I really am, at the center, is, first, no-thing, and then, later, everything. Doing the tube experiment with Harding last October really gave me the view that what I was, what I was looking out of, was essentially a featureless space. But my mind (read: ego, individuality-sense) couldn't accept the implications. The progression from there is captured in my isolation notes better than I can remember it. The jump to everythingness came as a result of seeing that I created every thing, and these things—mountains, people, etc.—are merely ghostly images that I am projecting on myself, on this blank screen.

The Love that we're looking for is the Love that comes with realizing our true identity.

(About ten days later, AP had a breakthrough. She said the phrase "Don't worry too much about the words... the important thing is to pick up a feeling" was on her mind when she awoke in the middle of the night. And then the thought crept up "I wonder what God feels like?" That was the key that opened the door.)

Does the Mind See?

Does the mind see the true self? Is it only through inquiry, or is there also a spontaneous recognition that "sees"?

Realization is spontaneous in the sense that the mind-self can't do it. Whether the mind-self's efforts help or hurt, my bias is toward the former. Whether inquiry or surrender is more effective, my bias is toward a combination. When realization occurs, the mind-self sees enough to lose its existential angst.

What would you be prepared to do if I answered "yes" to the first question? "No" to the first question? "Yes" to part "a" of the second question? "No" to part "a" of the second question? "Yes" to part "b" of the second question? "No" to part "b" of the second question?

If you answered "yes" to the first question I would attempt to "see" with my mind. How is that possible? It isn't. The mind's "job" is inquiry—in this way the mind is a tool and not as much of an "obstacle." I believe the quote: "Man has become a tool of his tools" is somewhat relevant. If you answered "no," I would have "gotten" to the second part of my answer. "Yes" to the second question results in "effortless" meditation as a valuable tool.

Effortless meditation is becoming conscious of the mind's activity from a semi-detached perspective. Self-inquiry is a reaction of the mind's intention to consciously try to find its source.

The mind's job—using the term broadly to include both thought and feeling—is also love, isn't it? Loving another, we put that other's welfare ahead of our own if necessary.

We sacrifice some personal luxury to buy something for a loved one, we sacrifice our body by throwing it on a grenade to save our buddies, etc. Inquiry plus surrender? Inquiry for the doer, surrender for the lover?

~ Art

Overwhelmed

The overwhelmed-by-the-world feeling I sometimes get has got to play some role in my psychology when I don't feel it. I fear it because of its strong conviction state, and right now I think I fear it could hold true for Dan. I try stepping back by trying to see my headlessness, but the emotion mostly continues, perhaps only 5% reduced. I normally think of seekers as having only weak emotional reactions/convictions and sometimes feel I need to aim for that or else I haven't reached some level of self-knowledge. I do have curiosity about the emotions, so perhaps acting on that is the point. But I also wonder if reducing emotional reactions isn't in itself important—watching as much as possible is what matters. So my question is, which is it? (And what is going on with that reaction?!?)

If your intuition tells you it is so, or if you can take a friend's word for it, finding out what we truly are solves all our existential problems. So the operant question becomes: "What can I do to find my true identity?"

You're probably familiar with the idea that where the eye goes, the heart follows.[39] We find our identity by looking within, and that looking takes us back to where there is no split between observer and observed. How that final transition

---

39 I found two translations that apparently come from Sanskrit writings:
a) "Where the hand goes, the eye follows; where the eye goes the mind follows; where the mind goes, the heart follows, and thus is born expression."
b) "Where the hand goes, the eye follows; where the eye goes, the mind goes; where the mind goes, is the heart; where the heart is, lies the reality of being."

happens will remain, in my opinion, a mystery... beyond knowing. In retrospect, we see that the observing-us became detached from identifying with what it was observing. The mind's hypnosis burned out or blew out. Don't try to see your headlessness or any other picture that you've heard described. Look for your true identity, whatever that may be.

The emotional conviction of being overwhelmed by the world results from a conviction state that formed early in your life. When you get some insight into the underpinnings of that state of mind, you'll see how it rests on beliefs about self and other. Mere beliefs... not absolute truth. As you observe reaction patterns of mind and body, you may see reactions to the reactions, which are determinations to see the primary reaction patterns change. Sometimes they will, and other times they won't. The important determinant of success in finding your true nature is that at some point the mind will tire of games, and it will turn and face the truth.

Having experienced that turning and facing of the truth, I was amazed at a line of advice given by a psychologist to a troubled FBI agent in an episode of the "Numb3rs" TV series a few years ago: "If you want to feel better, take a pill. If you want to get right, face the truth."

~ Art

Evolution of a Seeker

We feel that we are separate, individual, suffering beings who are incomplete within. We spend our lives trying to find a way to distract ourselves from this incompleteness/separateness by trying desperately to be complete. The next day always holds a promise of better than today.

Relationships, work, drugs, alcohol, etc. are what we use to try to keep ourselves occupied enough so that we somehow don't have to feel this inner angst. Pretty soon, if we are a bit introspective, we realize that no amount of blaming the universe for our suffering or looking for a solution outside will cure our misery. This is when we start to read self-help books, learn to meditate / pray, feel we are becoming more spiritual... basically trying to cope with life. Depending on what our circumstances have been, we may find ourselves turning to spiritualism. We all have some sort of relationship with the higher power... most of the time it is a father-god sitting somewhere watching over us. If you are from the east, you know God is everywhere but you just can't see it yet. You try to give It form, describe Its attributes and make temples for It.

Where we look
By now you have probably given religion/isms a shot and gone through different self-help programs where each promises a happy life once you follow that program regularly and honestly. After you spend a lot of time and money checking out such programs, you realize that they may not be the solution. Now you start to check out gurus who are popular. If you are lucky, you may find a real teacher who wants to

help you for the sake of helping you. If a guru is dependent on you for his bread and butter and has good selling skills, then probably you'll be paying for his lifestyle for a while.

Some of us try to use our intellect to get to Truth. We study scriptures, books, and what others have said in depth. We spend years trying to refine our understanding of the Truth. And one day it dawns on us that no matter how much we try to understand, the mind cannot put its arms around Truth. Intellectual understanding of what the book is talking about, or someone else's experience, cannot do it for you. You realize the emptiness of these profound words for you. You are again left in a quandary of what to do, where to go.

At this point, the mind starts to get a feel for 'looking within'… we start to observe ourselves. Your center of gravity moves from outside to within you. And by now you realize that spirituality is no more your favorite hobby, something you like to talk about, a morning/evening 20-minute meditation routine… it becomes a way of life.

What we do
We try to perfect our meditation technique or other techniques; look for answers in the scriptures, books, lectures. Eventually you come to the realization that the only thing that is getting in between you and You is you. As Alfred Pulyan says, it is the penny that blocks the sun. You wonder how you can remove yourself from being in the way. The interest/love for 'self' seems to be your root obstacle. No matter how you hold your head, your hypnotic involvement with this self and the universe does not get broken.

What we become
As we keep looking, though we may have heard this a thousand times before, it finally gets registered in the mind that the answers lie within. But how does one go inside? No matter

how hard you try, you realize, you are still looking outwards. The physical world, your body, thoughts, emotions... everything seems to be in your view... so, of course, it can't be you. The viewer cannot be the view. The simple process of self-observation starts to make obvious your self-centricity. Ego is just not pride; you realize it is the individual, special me that takes ownership of all life. It manifests as the doer. It dawns upon you that all that you know of yourself as who you are is nothing else but this ego... as soon as you say 'I'... it is the ego. Ego/self has finally realized that the only way to find anything that is Eternal is if it gets out of its own way. It is the ultimate act to survive. So how does ego get out of the way?

You realize the one who wants this enlightenment is nothing else but the ego, the very ego which keeps us from realizing our true nature. This is when I feel even the desire to find It sort of loses its importance. But nothing else makes you want to get out of bed. The only seemingly meaningful action you feel is when you do something / remember what your goal is / was. You are a monk within, you realize.

What did Mr. Rose mean by 'egoless vector'? This is it.

What we find
The observer, which initially seems to be active, becomes more and more passive. You get to a point where you feel you are in a wait mode... but you can't stop yourself from trying though you know whatever you 'do' will not take you there. But you keep trying... going to the next meeting, retreat, talk. Each book that you open, you hope may flick your switch. You want to go through life with the lightest steps possible, don't want to raise a single speck of dust. Inwardly, you keep trying to swim towards the shore, though you have no idea if you'll ever make it or if you are moving in the right direction... as Shawn Nevins says.

And then in a moment of pure intent, you simply want to know for the sake of knowing... and the gates of heaven open. Source, where all the creation / destruction happens, witnesses itself. It is where whatever one can imagine originates. There is nothing of you. You are That. And All is realized.

You still may not know everything, but all your questions are answered, all fears taken care of, no more pain from the illusion of being a separate entity. You finally know Thou art That... and it is not an intellectual understanding but a Direct Experience, a Direct Knowledge.

The physical body may still be going through its normal aches and pains and emotions and confusions, but you know you are Freedom... always aware of the Screen where the movie is playing out. God is.

~ Anima

5
Identity

Slippery Eel

Ego — what we feel ourselves to be — is a slippery eel, says Alfred Pulyan.[40]

I got to read Alfred Pulyan's letters to Richard Rose, for our self-inquiry/accountability email group report, in 2001 for the first time. He seems to hammer it in that our ego is what keeps us from Truth. Rumor was that Alfred Pulyan could transmit enlightenment through his letters. In my opinion, the magic lay in his ability to bring his student's attention to the ego. According to him, the ego is "the penny that blocks the sun." That statement really stopped me in my tracks. When I started looking for "my" ego... I realized I didn't really have a clear picture of what ego meant. Here are some insights I got about what ego could be:

- "He/She has a big ego"... I had heard this often. Ego meant being prideful, arrogant, conceited, superior or better than others. I had also heard the terms self-centered, selfish, full of herself, etc., which I equated with ego.

- As I started to notice what ego could be, I found that the one who was trying to figure out what ego could be was ego itself. All my life activity was proclaimed by ego.

- Anything that I could say as "I" or "me" or "my" originated in my ego, it seemed. Everything in my life... thoughts, feelings, emotions, actions, my story, I realized was ego manifesting.

---

40 See https://www.spiritualteachers.org/alfred-pulyan/ and http://www.selfdiscoveryportal.com/Pulyan.htm/.

Identity

- Survival by maintaining its felt position at the center of the universe is the main strategy of ego.
- Ego takes ownership.
- Ego maintains its specialness and uniqueness by feeling either superior or inferior to its neighbor. Ordinariness or indifference is not acceptable to the ego.
- Who is this that seeks Enlightenment? Who is this that is trying to get rid of ego and is seeking a higher Self? I had this notion that there is some inner/deeper me which was really beyond ego. But It is just the ego becoming more sophisticated and hiding in a cloak of spirituality now. It is playing the Master Game.[41]
- Pulyan calls it ego 1 and ego 2.
- The organism's desire for the permanent end of its suffering gets stronger than its desire for centricity.
- How do I get myself out of the way? Since I couldn't see anything other than ego when I looked within, I couldn't chop off my own head.
- I (the ego), decided that I will try to be indifferent to the ego's desires and wishes. Desire for enlightenment also was coming from ego, so I thought I will not gratify my ego by seeking.
- Life got much more livable as I started to step aside.
- The seeker-ego is most cunning and hardest to see.
- All our spiritual practices and seeking are going in circles if we do not recognize the real obstacle.
- The ego will never feel it is ready/good enough... the trick is to start noticing how ego keeps itself at the

---

41 *The Master Game*, by Robert S. de Ropp.

center and what can be done to get yourself out of the way.
- The very "I"-thought is ego... it can't be caught.
- The only way ego really gets eliminated is when it gets transcended.
- When ego-centricity gets removed, Self becomes evident.
- As Art says... first ego had him, now he has the ego.
- When you find your true Identity, your Source, then ego gets seen for what it is... a concept.

~ Anima

Self-Definition

What strikes me: "We cannot define a dimension except from another dimension. Thought cannot be defined in terms of thought."[42] What does he mean by "to define" here? Surely I can define my concept of a chair in terms of other concepts, like I do when I look up the dictionary. Is self-definition something other than everyday definitions of things?

It may require a lot of thinking to get the point Richard Rose was trying to get across, which—like getting the concept of X, "the unknown value" in algebra—comes through intuition. Some kids get the concept easily, others after a great deal of struggle, and some never.

We know intuitively what "chair" means. But what if we had to get the concept of chair across to someone who had no experience of chair-ness? We might start by saying: "It's something to sit on," to which the person might respond: "Oh, a carpet," or "Oh, a rock"—if they even knew what we meant by sitting. So we might then elaborate by saying, "No, it's not a carpet, and it's not a rock; it's something with four legs and a back that allows us to sit comfortably." We couldn't adequately define a chair to someone who didn't know what a chair is by sticking with analogy. It would require also defining it in terms of what it's not. In other words, definition requires comparison with opposites. That's the way the mind is structured. In fact, the mind can't conceive of something that is both X and not X at the same time. We have to somehow convey a perspective of what something is from "above" that thing (and similarities) and its opposites.

---

42   From *Psychology of the Observer*, by Richard Rose.

Self-definition is a dynamite term that gets at knowing the self. The mind tries to know itself by studying itself, but it turns out to be an impossible task. We can only know the mind by seeing it from a perspective that's above/behind the mind. When that occurs, we find ourselves beyond the constraints of relative knowing... the only "place" where absolute knowing occurs.

There's only one knowing that is certain beyond doubt, and that is self-knowing.

~ Art

Process Observer

"*The Process Observer really came into self-consciousness of itself, only after observations of processes were transcended, and Process Observer was witnessed from another mental plane.*"[43] This sentence is confusing; if it came into self consciousness of itself, and was witnessed from another mental plane... doesn't that mean it's seen from another plane, and so it's different, so how can it be said to be self-conscious?

That sounds like the kind of argument that a mutual friend [who will remain anonymous here] puts forth. When he first started coming to the Pittsburgh meetings a few years back, he and I would have long & intense arguments about minutiae. It finally dawned on me that his mental patterns were like mine used to be. When I recognized that pattern from having witnessed it in my own psychology, I described it to him, and that neutralized most of the arguing between us. I suspect in my case that I sensed my father's disapproval or non-acceptance of me[44] before I had the ability to conceptualize anything about it... and that my intellect developed as a way to feel superior to him, as I grew older. A more general possibility might be that feelings were overwhelming to me as a child, and the intellect developed as a defensive mechanism. In any case, people rightly accused me of having a mind like a steel-trap. The threat of being wrong overlaid the specter of annihilation, which I think all fears are rooted in.

---

43 From *Psychology of the Observer*, by Richard Rose.
44 In fairness to my long-deceased father, he always treated me with the utmost respect, support and love.

That was a long-winded preamble, eh? It amazes me that women [including the questioner] don't pick up on the fact that with Richard Rose's writing you have to read between the lines. [In other words, I think women tend to be more intuitive than men, myself included.] His often-convoluted wording is an indication, I think, of how his intellect—powerful as it was—couldn't match his intuition.

I think what he was trying to point to (just a guess on my part) is that when you get beyond the process observation point, the mind structure gets exceedingly hazy, as he said in other contexts. It's getting closer to the still non-space from which all manifestation arises. The closer you get to that, the less ponderable manifestation becomes—like going out into space or down into matter. The mind can't "understand" what he's trying to say about the further reaches of the mind, but he's trying to leave some tracks that another searcher may recognize, at least in retrospect.

I've heard quite a few people say blithely, after reading the *Psychology of the Observer*, oh yeah, I'm definitely a process observer. I never experienced any view that I described to myself-the-seeker as for-sure that of the process observer.

Rose was attempting to construct, after his experience, what has always struck me as the most beautiful metaphor I've ever encountered... of the "Jacob's ladder" climb taking us back to our source. The pregnant feeling between the words points to something more wonderful than what the mind can conceive of.

~ Art

Promise

Rustle of leaves
Under her feet
Trees almost bare
Chill in the air
Distant chimes of the gong
Shepherd hums his song

She walks up the hill
Her favorite rock is still

Crisp morning outside
Dark night inside
Beaten and chained
Pain ingrained

Eagle soaring in the sky
Deep valley holding a promise
Of freedom
Catches her eye

~ Anima

Maniram's Pets

Towns in the 70s were still small in India. The population outburst that you see today was far from imagination. Being the second most populated country, now you only see concrete buildings and humans. Kanwali, a small village, surrounded by the Shivalik Hills, at the bank of River Yamuna, had about 500 homes.

The house with the big mango orchard was where Tinnie lived with her grandparents. Skinny Tinnie, as her friends from kindergarten called her, had big mischievous eyes. Her disheveled long curly hair, spilling out of her two long braids tied with red ribbons at the end, couldn't be controlled.

Harsh, cold winter had finally given way to spring. Trees had started to show budding life. The beautiful sunny day still had a little chill in the air. Tinnie, back from school, was now playing in her yard. Mischief maker, as her grandma called her, she loved to climb the low branches of tall mango trees. She sometimes hid in there and played with her imaginary friends. Sitting on a high branch, swaying her legs, she ignored her grandma's call, "come inside for lunch, Tinnie." Suddenly her ears perked up as she heard that familiar sound of the Been[45] getting closer. She knew it was her friend Maniram, the snake charmer, heading in her direction. This made her jump from the tree and run across the orchard towards the gate.

This tall, dark and lean man, dressed in a long white shirt and Lungi,[46] wore a big colorful turban on his head. His

---

45 A wind instrument played by snake charmers, also called the pungi and the murli.
46 Traditional Indian pants.

black kohled eyes seemed to be smiling all the time. He wore earrings and necklaces made of beads around his neck. He walked the streets with sacks hanging from two ends of a bamboo pole on his shoulders. The sacks contained wicker baskets—resting space for his pet snakes.

Catching snakes and making them perform on the streets was Maniram's source of livelihood, a profession that he inherited from his forefathers. Maniram often wandered around, visiting small towns and villages during market days and festivals. He would set up his stage on an open ground. His audience would gather around in a circle while he made his pet reptiles dance to his tunes.

Been, an instrument made of dried gourd, was how he played music for his snakes. This hypnotized the snakes, and they seemed drunk. Though snakes do not have ears, they danced to the visual cue of the swaying pipe. Ground vibrations caused by his tapping feet also led them to their next move.

There was a time when Tinnie used to be scared of Maniram and his snakes. She would try to hide whenever she heard Maniram's Been. Lollipops and Maniram's gentle cajoling soon got him on her list of friends.

The two exchanged smiles as their eyes met. "How was school, little girl," asked Maniram while looking for a place to set up for his snake performance. "I don't like school," Tinnie replied. The deep conversation between the two went on regarding school and the advantages of going or not going to school.

Hearing Maniram's Been, people started to trickle in from the nearby market. The thing about small towns is that nobody is ever in a hurry to get anywhere. Life moves at an extremely slow pace while drinking tea and smoking cigarettes.

Tinnie loved the stories Maniram narrated about his snakes. He pulled out seven tightly closed baskets from his sack. The first basket he opened had a vine snake in it. "His name is Haria (means green-colored in Hindi), shown through his slender body, which is perfect for him as he lives on trees and eat frogs." Maniram got Haria wrapped around his arm and took it close to the crowd. "This is not poisonous," assured Maniram. Tinnie touched the scaly skin of the snake with her tiny fingers.

The other snakes that he pulled out were mostly non-venomous. Each one had a name. There was a rattlesnake, venomous, called Drums; an Indian rat snake, supposed to be really fast, named Mousey; a trinket snake, slender and medium-sized, called Bali; and then a light colored snake named Blondie.

The last two baskets were relatively bigger than the other ones. Curious Tinnie wanted Maniram to open them next. "Have patience, little girl!" Maniram said. Nag and Nagina, black Cobras, were his star performers. One of the most venomous snakes, they were the latest additions to his collection. He had caught them from a nearby field. He mentioned that these have not been defanged yet. Snake charmers break the front two teeth to make the snakes non-poisonous.

Maniram seemed extra cautious when he loosened the lid of the next basket. Bright black on top and light colored at the bottom, the two snakes lay coiled up together. Maniram nudged them with the front of his Been. Suddenly one of the snakes raised its proud head up. It had a spectacle pattern on its hood. It thrust its tongue out with a hiss. The crowd cheered and applauded. This was the female cobra, Nagina. Her head swayed from side to side with the sway of Maniram's Been. Nag, the male, was still refusing to budge out of his coil. Maniram took his Been closer to the basket

Identity

and continued playing till Nag lazily started to slither out. The crowd suddenly got quiet, bewitched by the beauty of the black reptile.

Maniram, hands covered with thick mittens, caught Nag before he could slide away into the crowd. He caught the snake by his neck and made him open his mouth by sticking his fingers on the side of his mouth, pointing out the poisonous fangs. Snakebite releases the venom in the victim's body. It spreads with the blood and acts on the nerves, paralyzing muscles. Respiratory or cardiac arrest causes death within twenty minutes. "So don't get too close to snakes," said Maniram in his matter of fact voice.

Pleased with all the money Maniram collected from the cheering crowd that day, he also sold some herbs and pain medicines. Tinnie hung around Maniram while he started to collect his stuff. He patiently answered her questions about what snakes ate, where they slept and if baby snakes were also poisonous. She asked him to bring a snake baby next time for her to play with. Maniram laughed and told her snakes are not toys... even when they are little. He cautioned her to stay away and run if she saw one.

It was already summer and still no sign of Maniram. He usually visited town once a month. He lived with his wife and three sons in the nearby village. Tinnie was wondering when Maniram is going to come next. She asked her grandmother if they could go and visit him in his village. She got an assurance that Maniram will be coming soon to perform at the fair.

Today when Tinnie returned from school, she sensed something was not right at the house. Her grandparents looked serious sitting in their lawn chairs as she entered the gate. After the initial hustle and bustle of how the school went, her grandmother in a quiet voice mentioned that Maniram got bitten by Nag. Tinnie's little heart suddenly missed a beat. "Is he in the hospital?" she asked. "No, Maniram was found dead in his bed," replied her grandfather. "Dead and bed rhymes," thought Tinnie as she sat in her grandmother's lap and put her head on her chest. Apparently, Nag managed to get out of his basket, climbed up Maniram's bed and bit him while he was sleeping. His family found the bite marks on Maniram's leg. Nag was nowhere to be found.

Nobody has called me Tinnie ever since my grandmother passed away.

~ Anima
(True story except for the names of the characters.)

Loss of Self

I am unsure about myself in that I feel I'm an unsure person. I'm often unsure about what I want (I can't define what I want exactly), unsure about whether I'm loved, unsure about my abilities, etc. I want to know these things so I can be a sure person, but to me it is not the same as self-knowing. Yes, I cannot conceive of defining something without knowing its opposites. So to me, defining my self is further separating myself from other things until I get this distinct, discrete me... a disconnected something. Lately I want to feel more connected.

I know I want to know, but I don't know what it is exactly I want to know about (forgive me, I don't mean it as a play of words). But I came to Pittsburgh (school) because I was going to get serious at knowing (life intellectually), but before school even began, I met you, and I was convinced that you "know," that you have something I want. It always attracts me when I perceive sure (maybe even absolute) knowing in someone—it happened only twice, actually. How do I make this desire productive? How can I begin to answer if I don't define what it is exactly that I want to know?

You're over-thinking. You "know" (i.e., feel) that you want to be loved, but you're afraid to pursue it because rejections are painful. Real love involves loss of self—temporarily in lesser cases (falling in love with Jesus, or another person, for example). You're afraid of loss of self. That's the main contradiction or war your mind-self may be grappling with.

Dear God, I see it.... It is very true.... What do I?

Always Right Behind You

The entire path to Truth / Self / Completion is through admitting the truth of what we see. Once the mind-self has admitted the truth of something it has seen about itself, it can move on... i.e., continue watching the war within until the contestants are all dead or only One remains.

~ Art

The Ego

The final, most obstinate, and most wily of all obstructions to crossing the finish line to Nirvana is the ego. The ego is not:

- Pride ("He's a proud fellow, struts around like a rooster").
- Selfishness ("She only thinks of herself").
- Narcissism ("He's in love with himself").
- Something to school, polish or perfect.
- Something to try to minimize or to kill off.

The ego is not a collection of our negative attributes. The ego does have a game it likes to play, though, splitting the personality patterns into two camps: the "good" ones that it identifies with (me, the saint, the angel) and the "bad" ones that it disowns (not me, the devil made me do it, the sinner).

The ego is a belief planted in us by what created us — a belief that we're something (some thing).

The ego is the individuality-sense itself. It is the "I am" that identifies with certain forms, feelings and constructs:

- I am hungry.
- I am the guy in the mirror.
- I am the person who awakes in the morning and falls asleep at night.
- I am unhappy.

- I am the person who was born a certain number of years ago and will die at some uncertain time in the future.
- I am the person with this name and this set of personality traits and memories that make me unique.
- I am lovable.
- I am the individual body-mind that is separate from other body-minds and whose existence is threatened and subject to extinction.
- I am the spirit or soul that will survive the death of the body.

We view our life-experience through the sense-of-self. It is the innermost observer that we're identified with and is thus not something that comes into our view. So how can we observe it?

Richard Rose has the most practical, common-sense system for bringing this about that I've come across. The general outline is one of retreating from false identification (a process which Franklin Merrell-Wolff also touched on in his "Induction" talk). It's not a logical process that can be conducted by analysis or argument, but a process of introspective observation. A sample progression might go something like this:

- I *have* a body—which implies that it's not the innermost me.
- Similarly, I have thoughts and feelings—admittedly more interior possessions than my shirt and shoes, but still not me.

Identity

- I can scrutinize the beliefs and convictions that run my life, thus putting them more consciously into my view, where I realize they, too, are possessions (or obsessions).
- I can view my decision-making process—first indirectly, by looking at the results, and then directly—seeing that this process is part of the mind's automatic machinery that functions regardless of whether I'm aware of watching it or not. I see that I'm not "the decider," and yet I insist that I'm the final arbiter.
- I can see that I'm not "the doer," since action results from thought, which has already happened when I become aware of it. Yet despite lack of control, I try to be in control. After all, what would happen if I just gave up?
- I can view and review my defensive reactions when I feel threatened—anger, sarcasm, lashing out, withdrawal, arguing, feeling superior, feeling hurt, shocked, rejected, looking for comfort, replaying events in my imagination and having them come out differently, planning revenge, and so on. These are afflictions to the individuality-sense and therefore clues to its existence and whereabouts.
- As Merrell-Wolff sums it up: "I'm not the mind, I'm not the feelings, I'm not the body—that I see. But I surely *am*, I surely am an individual, apart from others."

This sense of being something apart is the ego. Eventually there is a direct seeing into what we're looking out from and a realization that the only observer is the Observatory.

~ Art

How Do You Relate to Me?

Are you wondering why I am telling you these random stories? I have yet to come across a story, a book, a movie that I have not liked or found interesting. This is one of my favorites since it helped me see my relationship with the higher Self.

This is a dialogue between Rama[47] and Hanuman:[48]

> Once Rama asked Hanuman, "How do you relate to me, Hanuman?"
>
> Hanuman replied. "When I am conscious of this body-mind, Rama, you are my lord, and I am your servant. I worship you.
>
> When I am conscious of my being-ness, individual soul, I am part of You. You are the Whole.
>
> When I am conscious of Self, then You and I are One. This is my firm conviction."

~ Anima

---

47   Incarnation of Vishnu; hero of the *Ramayana* epic.
48   Monkey God, devotee of Rama.

Dead Particles

Hair: dead particles of protein being pushed out of the body.
Thoughts/feelings: dead particles of neural energy being pushed out of the mind.
Both: have practical uses for the body during its temporary survival.
But: how many of us become attached to egos (little selves) concerning the body's hair or the mind's thoughts and feelings?
Love 'em or hate 'em, sometimes flipping back and forth,
Chasing or fleeing the desires, fearing or blessing the fears,
Impressed with our self-identifications or mortified by them.
What is the real value of the body-mind or its products in the quest for Real Life?

~ Art

Elusion
Corina Bardasuc

I turn around and round
The self
Like a dog
Chasing its own tail.
Trying to sniff out
My very soul.
My senses lead me
Astray
Most of the time.
My hearing wasted
On the song of birds.
My taste sense wasted
On many hardened bones.
My eyes hardened
By the chase of many fleeting
Things.
But yesterday I think,
When I was circling yet
Again,
I caught the scent
Of a thought.
Unlike the other thoughts.
It simply told me
Stop.

Homage to Love

Two heads on a pillow
We lose ourselves in each other's eyes
And feel the oneness of love.

I bow in allegiance to you, O Lord
Creator of the universe of love and hate
And misunderstood ruler thereof.

And bowing to you I lose my head
And losing my head I am no longer the I of the body
And bowing my headlessness I am no longer the I of the mind.

But I am still here
But I and Thou are no longer two
But the melding of zero and infinity.

Love is a feeling
Love is oneness becoming twoness
Love is twoness becoming oneness.

But Love is Identity
And Love is our Home.

~ Art

Feet of Clay

You found that your lover had clay feet:[49]
You're let down, angry,
Hoping, believing, you'd found unconditional love this time.

Is it possible that unconditional love in this dimension
Simply manifests as acceptance of what is....
Not undiscriminating liking of what is,
Not benevolent non-reaction?

If your clayness could experience unconditional love
Would it dispense with the struggle
To *become* unconditioned love?

~ Art

---

49 "Thou, O king, sawest... a great image.... This image's head was of fine gold, his breast and his arms of silver, his belly and his thighs of brass, his legs of iron, his feet part of iron and part of clay." (*Daniel* 2:31-33)

Productive Mood

𝒟id you feel that way, about [depression] being productive, at the time or in retrospect.

I think we can only make a true assessment of our state of mind in retrospect. Once we stop resisting whatever life has thrown at us, we can truly start to see the value in that life-lesson... sort of taking a step back from whatever the situation is and getting a bigger view in your consideration. The only problem with having a dominant mood would be that any situation is colored by it... this is where the group work / friends may help... to keep your perspective straight.

Please clarify this mystifying statement [you made last time]:

> I used to think I was looking for God/Truth but basically I just wanted freedom from my suffering... which I found much sooner than I found God... but then I realized that wasn't going to cut it for me... So my friend, if freedom from suffering is your goal then you'll find it very-very easily as you walk this path.

Very easily found? Before awakening?

Sure... you see, I found my suffering was directly proportional to my self-centricity/humongous EGO. As my sense of 'self/ego' shrank, so did my suffering. ☺ And then I got to the point where my suffering was no more a motivator but I had no other life goals / desires left either.

Self-Inquiry I have found to be the most direct and straight path to finding my-Self.

And when you do Awaken, you may be surprised that how little it has to do with all these oh-so-big reasons we all have for looking for It. You still will find yourself chopping wood and drawing water. ☺

~ Anima

Purpose and Benefit

M: *Do you think your "purpose" in life was to wake up? Do you think Life had any other purpose for you? Do you think everyone's purpose is to wake up?*

AP: Yes, and I wasn't going to leave any stone unturned… though I knew that it wasn't any system or organization that would resolve my problem. I guess I was looking for ways to at least reduce my angst/pain. I don't think I have ever taken a single wasteful breath. Whatever I did was what I needed to do in that moment.

❧

M: *Were you ever a curious person?*

AP: Curiosity is an integral part of human programming… yes, I was… I still am.

❧

Anima: You'll be surprised, Mary, but most people do not want to talk about spiritual stuff.

M: *I found that out a long time ago. Sigh. Do you think there is any benefit to awakening? Is it something you would want for your children?*

AP: Are you kidding me… why would I want even a single sentient being to be living in a dark cell, in bondage? Each being also has its own blueprint to live by. Living only happens after Awakening.

※

M: *I still don't understand why realizing you are the Only One would be a good thing. Maybe it's a trick!*

AP: Wow... this is an interesting perspective... do you think this is why One splits itself into many?

※

M: *If this is what you want for your children, is it something you would encourage them to consider? Or are you hoping that eventually, they will ask about it?*

AP: Can you ever rest in peace without knowing who you are, knowing your real identity?
   The very nature of life, with death dangling in front, is a great encouragement for all.

~ Anima

Tough Love

Nobushige, a great samurai, sought out Hakuin[50] and asked: "Is there really a heaven and a hell?"
"Who are you?" asked Hakuin.
"I am a samurai," Nobushige replied.
"You?" Hakuin snorted. "What lord would employ you? You look like a beggar!"
A furious Nobushige began to draw his sword, but then Hakuin said, "Here open the gates of hell."
Nobushige took the point, sheathed his sword, and bowed.
"Here open the gates of heaven," said Hakuin.

~ Art

Hakuin, *Two Blind Men on a Log Bridge*

---

50 Hakuin Zenji was a tough-minded Japanese Zen master in the 1700s. He also used art to teach the dharma, creating thousands of ink and paint drawings and calligraphies. He depicted Mobius strips a century before Mobius "invented" them and predated Escher with his paintings within paintings.

6

Is There an End?

When Flame Was a Flower

Francesco Bernadone was an impetuous young man who responded to a call to arms when his city went to war with a neighboring city in 1202 AD. He and his contingent were captured, he became sick, and continued recovering at home after being ransomed by his father. There he dreamed a vision of an armory where all the arms were emblazoned with the sacred cross... and took this as a call to join a papal war in Sicily. But a little way along the road his sickness took over.

He then had a second dream, this time with a voice telling him he had mistaken the meaning of the vision and telling him to return to his home. There he descended into humiliation over his failure. On a ride outside the city walls as he was recovering his health, probably in 1204, he saw a figure coming toward him on the road and halted... confronted with a great fear:

> He was riding listlessly in some wayside place, apparently in the open country, when he saw a figure coming along the road towards him and halted; for he saw it was a leper. And he knew instantly that his courage was challenged, not as the world challenges, but as one would challenge who knew the secrets of the heart of a man. What he saw advancing was not the banner and spears of Perugia, from which it never occurred to him to shrink; nor the armies that fought for the crown of Sicily, of which he had always thought as a courageous man thinks of mere vulgar danger. Francis Bernadone saw his fear coming up the road towards him; the fear that comes from within and not without, though it stood white and horrible in the sunlight. For

once in the long rush of his life his soul must have stood still. Then he sprang from his horse, knowing nothing between stillness and swiftness, and rushed on the leper and threw his arms around him. It was the beginning of a long vocation of ministry among many lepers, for whom he did many services; to this man he gave what money he could and mounted and rode on. We do not know how far he rode, or with what sense of the things around him, but it is said that when he looked back, he could see no figure on the road.

That vignette comes from a biography of *St. Francis of Assisi* by G.K. Chesterton. Francis became a self-imposed mendicant and a *bhakti* devotee of Jesus whose passion attracted others to a way of living lives of poverty, chastity and obedience — an informal brotherhood that became the Order of Friars Minor.

Francis may have experienced cosmic consciousness. Witnesses commonly reported that he radiated a love of all things, as Chesterton relates in this illustration:

> When he was about to preach in a wood full of the chatter of birds, he said, with a gentle gesture, "Little sisters, if you have now had your say, it is time that I also should be heard." And all the birds were silent, as I for one can very easily believe.

Chesterton also points out that Francis referred to the sun not just as Brother Sun but as *Monsieur notre frère*—"a phrase that one king might use of another."

In 1219 Francis made a trip to Egypt to try to convert the Muslims. He apparently contracted an eye disease that was painful and causing him to go blind. Back in Italy, friends convinced him to have his eyes cauterized. When the physician approached with a red-hot iron, Francis said:

Is There an End?

"Brother Fire, God made you beautiful and strong and useful; I pray you be courteous with me."

> He remembered the time when a flame was a flower, only the most glorious and gaily colored of the flowers in the garden of God, and when that shining thing returned to him in the shape of an instrument of torture, he hailed it from afar like an old friend, calling it by the nickname which might most truly be called its Christian name.

The flame of love is a flower, birds singing in the woods, the sun hurting Francis's eyes when he was going blind, Francis living with lepers... and lying "bare upon the bare ground, to prove that he had and that he was nothing" in his death agony—where "the stars which passed above that gaunt and wasted corpse stark upon the rocky floor had for once, in all their shining cycles round the world of laboring humanity, looked down upon a happy man."

~ Art

Buddha Nature
Richard Rose

The Buddha-nature to me is nothing more than the vein of the absolute that's in every human being. But what will it take for it to be conscious, for the person to be conscious of it? What it amounts to basically, I maintain, is that everybody is unconscious; and when a person realizes the Buddha-nature then the small-s self and the large-s Self are both conscious of each other for the first time.[51]

---

[51] From part 2 of a talk, "Relative and Absolute," given at Ohio State University in 1978; https://tatfoundation.org/forum2020-04a.htm#6/.

Where Is the Path?

I thought I knew exactly what I wanted out of life, but I think that knowing was intellectual, i.e. what else could make more sense than to want to be permanently free of (existential) suffering? Emotionally, however, I've been drawn towards love (between myself and a woman), which indicates an unconscious belief in temporal love being the answer for me.

I don't appear to have the patience for temporal love. When things do "line up" between me and a woman, it is for a brief period. But surrounding that brief period of fulfillment is an experience of total identification with the object of my desire. I almost lose my sense of self when I contemplate my "beloved."

But intellectually, I know that "this is not it." But it is also hard to find the determination within myself to keep pushing inward, when my experience is one of having lost a big part of myself. I am simply not aware of something bigger within myself. What I take myself to be is more-or-less a beheaded chicken, still doing its aimless dance (I'm sure there is still pride left in there somewhere, because if I were truly beheaded, then there would be a greater sense of collapse/disillusionment).

I hope the above makes some sense. And it's probably also easy to guess, from what I've said, that I have lost someone I loved profoundly.

I see how I didn't end up asking a specific question. What I am looking for is perspective. If God wants me to find Him, and he's merely pushing me in the right direction, why don't I have any sense (or evidence) of the Path for me?

Where to start? Let's go back to the beginning. Elton John nailed it in the haunting lines from one of his songs: "There was a time / I was everything and nothing / all in one." Maybe a glimpse from an acid trip? It's what the song of silence, the vibration of the umbilical cord connecting the mind to its source, is telling us. The mind-self emanates from paradise and wants to find what it feels has been lost, or what it feels cut off from in its isolation cell. The mind operates in a time-bound dimension, though, and doesn't know how to navigate its way back to timelessness. It comes out of timelessness into waking consciousness and goes back into timelessness on a regular basis, but it is semi-conscious at best of timelessness during the waking or dreaming states—seemingly stuck in its separation from paradise.

Falling in love is a good sign for the seeker of paradise… and a clue to the state of non-separation. The problem is that the mind-self isn't satisfied with one-way loving and wants, even more, to feel loved. And it wants to be loved unconditionally, which another mind-self isn't capable of. So sooner or later, falling in love leads to disappointment and disillusionment.

What is the mind-self's reaction to disappointment and disillusionment? It will either give up (pessimism) or keep struggling (optimism). Generally it swings back and forth between those two reactions.

When the mind-self sees (i.e., intuits) the impossibility of finding a truly permanent solution in the time-bound dimension, the only remaining possibility is to become conscious of where it comes from and goes back to. Whether that's possible falls into the domain of faith. Hubert Benoit[52] described the stages of the psychosomatic development of the child into the "natural" man and the reversal of those stages in the development of the man who becomes awake to his true state of being. The first of three preliminary openings he

---

52 In *The Supreme Doctrine: Psychological Studies in Zen Thought*

Is There an End?

described was that of the faith center, which occurs with the realization that the Creative Principle has not abandoned its creation and in fact has never stopped working for its benefit. I think intuition can reach the faith in something bigger than our mind-self through feelings, picking up the vibrations of the umbilical cord calling us Home, or through the intellect, which becomes conscious of the incomprehensible complexity of the cosmic creation and admits that there's some principle vastly more intelligent than itself running the operation.

As for the path, it's visible only in retrospect. Metaphorically, we can't walk into the light since it's blinding, but we back away from darkness and ignorance into the light.

~ Art

The Nature of Desire

The story goes that after Buddha got enlightened he started to look for the root cause of human suffering. One day he was passing through a forest and came across a colony of lepers. Since there was no cure for leprosy and it was considered a highly contagious disease, people who got leprosy could not be part of the regular society. They had to live away from the village. This disease causes skin lesions and nerve damage. He noticed that people suffered from this intense itch in their wounds. To stop the itch, they were putting coals on their wound. And yet the itch wouldn't stop; the wound got bigger and itched more. Buddha realized that this was the very condition of the human heart consumed by desire.

He found that human life is driven by the underlying desires and fears. Buddha concluded that the root cause of all suffering is desire. It causes that never-ending inner itch: no matter what you do, it never gets quenched.

Desire is like a fire.
The more you try to satisfy it, the stronger it gets. Its nature is such that it holds a promise of fulfillment but never gets satisfied. The carrot is always hanging in front, but you never can reach it. Even when you think you have found your carrot, desire transforms into a dangling grapefruit, ready to be chased.

Desire causes action.
If you look, nothing in this universe is out of line. Desire must be serving some important purpose in human life even when

perceived as the cause of suffering. In its simplest form, desire to live is programmed into all living things. It makes the seed grow. Single-celled bacteria and viruses know how to live and survive. It is the impetus for the organism to move. By its very nature desire is not meant to bring satisfaction. It causes action.

Desire gives direction.
How does desire play out in human life? Humans, being a little more evolved and complex than the rest of the living beings, make desire more complicated. Depending on the phase of life, desire manifests as a want for toys, love, control, and other objects with the promise of fulfillment at the end of the acquisition. A man enslaved by desire lives his life in its pursuit. Desires, unexamined, will keep you running like a hamster on a wheel.

On the other hand, if a man gets a conviction that what he desires he may not find, his will to live may go. There was once a very driven monk. He asked his teacher what his chances of finding enlightenment were. The teacher said that from what he has seen, chances of the monk getting enlightened were slim. The next morning the monk was found dead in his room.

Honest inquiry into what the heart really wants will at least give a direction to the inquirer. And when you have learned to discern where a particular desire will take you, you may have a window of opportunity to save yourself from meaningless pursuits that may cost you your lifetime, maybe more. After being driven by many desires, I finally learned to ask myself: "When I get XYZ, the object of my heart's desire, will that cure my dis-ease?" I realized no matter what road I would get on, it wouldn't resolve my inner suffering.

The Power of Desire.
Let me warn you, do not underestimate the power of desire. I have found it to be much stronger than human will or reason. You can't get rid of it. What your heart wants, it wants. If you examine it, you will find that you do not pick your desire; desire picks you. Logic may not be able to help you in ridding you of your desires. You can't fight it. Desire will win. Any attempt to control it only makes it stronger. However, I have found that the power of simple observation is such that the desire dissipates, no matter what the problem is. Observe, endure, and wait: that is how you ride out the storm.

Purification of Desire.
Though desire is associated with pleasure, at a deeper level, it is pointing towards a feeling of an inner lack. It gives hope of satisfaction when the object will be acquired. So no matter what the object is, if investigated, it will lead to the same revelation.

Now it is a simple matter of you asking yourself what does my heart really want that will end my suffering permanently?

"You are what your deep, driving desire is. As your desire is, so is your will. As your will is, so is your deed. As your deed is, so is your destiny."[53]

~ Anima

---

53 *Brihadaranyaka Upanishad* IV.4.5

Complete Surrender

Eric Liddell (rhymes with *riddle*) was a Scottish athlete and missionary. He was born in China in 1902 and returned there as a missionary in 1925, where he died in a Japanese internment camp in 1945 just months before the end of WWII.

He garnered the nickname of The Flying Scotsman, after the record-breaking locomotive of that name, when he was in school at Eltham College, a boarding school in England, and later at the University of Edinburgh.

His forte was the 100-meter event, but that event in the 1924 Summer Olympics was scheduled for a Sunday, and Eric's beliefs wouldn't let him race on Sunday. So he trained for the 400-meter event. He not only won the race but set a new world record.

By 1941, life in China was becoming dangerous due to the invasion by Japan's armies, so Liddell's wife and children left to stay with her family in Canada. In his last letter to his wife, on the day he died, he said he was suffering from a nervous breakdown, but it turned out to have been a brain tumor.

In 2008, before the Beijing Olympics, Chinese authorities revealed that he had the opportunity to leave the internment camp in a prisoner exchange arranged between the Japanese and British, but he gave his place to a pregnant woman. Typical of the man, whose headmaster in his boarding school had described him as "entirely without vanity," he hadn't told anyone about that sacrifice, which came as a surprise even to his family.

His running style toward the end of a race, with his head flung back and his mouth wide open, was portrayed in the film about his Olympic win, *Chariots of Fire*. He described that state one time, saying: "I believe that God made me for a purpose, but He also made me fast. When I run, I feel His pleasure."

A fellow missionary in the internment camp said that Liddell's last words were: "It's complete surrender."

~ Art

O Come, All Ye Faithful

There are those who have faith in Me
 but aren't good listeners.
And there are those who don't have faith in Me
 and refuse to hear Me.
Are you unsure of what direction to take,
 what option to choose?
I am the path to all that life has to offer,
 but you don't remember Me.
Thus speaks your inner self,
 the Love and the Answer that you're looking for.

~ Art

Craving, Longing, Yearning

*T*rying to get some clarity on these three confusing feelings...

Craving, as for something that (you think) will bring satisfaction or enjoyment. Craving implies a deep and imperative wish for something, based on a sense of need and hunger; craving for food, for companionship. Appetites are the main cause of cravings. More physical, as in I craved cinnamon buns when I was pregnant. Physical.

Longing is an intense wish, generally repeated or enduring, for something that is at the moment beyond reach but may be attainable at some future time; longing for home, nostalgia. Radha longs for Krishna to return; longing to go home. That little ache in your heart. Heartfelt.

Yearning suggests persistent uneasiness and sometimes wistful or tender longing. You yearn for that completion/ Love (as in unconditional love, acceptance; feeling of rest within and without). Meera's yearning in her bhajans. This is a being-felt feeling.

~ Anima

Understanding the Mind

With the experience where you realized you were nothing special, what proceeded it that made your mind open to accepting that? I tend to waver in my emotional conviction on this matter and suspect this ego causes me some grief.

Acceptance of my non-specialness was not at all easy, Dan. My story, personality, preferences, and everything that represented who I was, or that made me, were extremely special and unique according to me. But once you become a bit observant and start to notice what you are not, all these special events/things/attributes, etc., start to lose their importance, and you realize the freedom in being ordinary.

What do you make of the conflict of knowing I'm conscious vs being conscious? For Art and Phil this seemed to dominate their thinking until their minds stopped. If it weren't for their pointing it out repeatedly, I probably wouldn't keep trying to notice the contradiction. I can say they are different types of observation occurring, but not make the leap that I am 2 things.

Sorry, Dan... my psychology is such that it didn't worry about if I was conscious vs. being conscious. My mind doesn't ask too many questions or like complex concepts ☺, so statements like "I am That" or questions like "Who am I?" only made me very irritated because I felt clueless about what these meant. I just knew that the only thing between me and Me was me, and I had to get myself out of the way. And then I found that I am that Consciousness / Awareness. Duality is only in our mind. Mind is the tool that you can use wisely instead of becoming its slave.

Mind is conscious of objects. When you faint, mind loses consciousness. You have awareness of your consciousness. You are never *not aware*. Awareness is aware of itself.

That really resonated, especially the phrase "duality is only in the mind." Is the mind that which makes everything experienced?

Mind, to me, is just like any other organ in my body, but I think we are more identified with it than with our kidneys or lungs or stomach. It is the CPU of the machine-body. It is doing its job of churning out experience based on the program it is running, but it is important material to study because the mind is what we are most identified with. It is almost like studying mind with the mind to get to the point beyond the mind ☺.

~ Anima

Emotions

Can you tell us something about the role that your emotions played in relation to your search?

It is politically incorrect to ask a woman about her emotions. ☺ Shawn Nevins once gave a presentation about moods… he was taking some medication which was really playing havoc with his hormones. He admitted to how hard he thought it would be to be a woman because the moods (which get triggered by whatever the dominant hormone is) changed so often. ☺

But if you really are seeking Truth, then can you afford to let your ever-changing emotions and moods get in the way? By simply watching them come and go, you tend to short-circuit them. There is always a small window when you can avoid getting sucked into your stronger emotions before they consume you. And then some emotions, I found, were quite productive. I found that depression or a sad mood was not so bad because it made me want to sit and really look at what exactly was the pain about. When I was depressed, I didn't have enough energy or desire to go out and have fun; instead, I realized my mind became slower and life happened in slow motion. I had to actually sit and watch what exactly was going on within.

Nostalgia is another strong mood/emotion that makes one want to seek Home.

~ Anima

Loss of Everything

*C*haracteristically, as I have every intensive (this was my third), I suffer anxiety attacks and stark dreams about death afterwards. I call it the vertigo of death—nothing holding me, nothing beneath me—just dangling by the barest of threads above an abyss that I can never escape. And it is not that I might fall in some future time—even the feeling of the dangling is part of the falling—that there is no escape right now. The great sorrow that accompanies this is the loss of everything—particularly those whom I love. It is overwhelming. Phil said something about realizing that the individualized consciousness will not survive death, and that really stuck in [my] craw. That really gets me—because I see deep down, I really want to survive death somehow. This is still somehow a question for me that is really getting under my skin even if I can intellectually admit to impermanence or non survival.

Not to worry… the "everything" you now have is evanescent. The "everything" you become is forever.

We are not able to love fully while we believe ourselves to be individuals. The evaporation of that faulty belief allows us to BE love.

The first time I REALLY felt love was right after I came back into consciousness from my self-realization and felt the great poignancy of the life of the aged nun who was the guest director at the Benedictine monastery in Erie, PA where I did my final solitary retreat. She'd given her life to Jesus, dedicated it to God, not yet knowing that she IS what she's been looking for all her long life of dedicated service.

What you are doesn't die. You experience life and death, but you are eternal being, not something that comes and goes.

~ Art

No Room
Another View of Triangulation

There's no room to take in a new view
My dear, dear friend
When we're in love with the old view –
Because a new view opposes the old one.
There's no room to take in a stranger
My dearest, my love
When we're in love with the self –
Because an other opposes the loved one.
Love comes into the world of self
In a humble manger.

~ Art

Only...

In the absence of Suffering
Joy remains

in the absence of Pride
Humility remains

in the absence of Complexity
Simplicity remains

in the absence of Ignorance
Knowledge remains

In the absence of Pretense
Acceptance remains

in the absence of Desire
Equanimity remains

in the absence of Fear
Love remains

in the absence of Separation
Unity remains

in the absence of Object
Space remains

Is There an End?

in the absence of Thought
Awareness remains

in the absence of Ego
You remain

~ Anima

A Wave of Timelessness
Marjorie Kinnan Rawlings

Yesterday when I stood under the large pecan tree by the barn gate, the amnesia came over me. I had not expected a crop this year, for the trees bore heavily last season, and are almost completely biennial in their bearing. But as I reached absently to pull down a bough, I saw that slender green nuts were forming at the growth-ends of all the branches. The sight was unexpected, and I was suddenly lost in a wave of timelessness. I thought for an instant that I was back in the May of a year ago. Then it seemed to me that I had skipped this present season and had been precipitated into the coming year. The pecan tree was bearing again, and where was I in time and space? And the old comfort came, in the recurrence, and on the heels of the comfort, despair, that there was no end to seasons, but an end to me.[54]

---

54 *Cross Creek* by Marjorie Kinnan Rawlings.

Whirlwind

Like a whirlwind
he sweeps onto the stage;
like an entertainer
he dazzles the audience with his wit;
like a Lothario
he enchants the viewer with his charms…
feeling empty, empty all the while.

The curtain descends
and he feels exhausted,
reviewing his performance
to remove any imperfections…
but wondering why he has to work so hard
to find the appreciation he's needing,
the security he's seeking,
the love he longs for
and the peace he wordlessly prays for.

He doesn't yet see that
he's running away from
that which is pursuing him,
always right behind him,
offering all that his heart desires.

Some day,
some hour,
some moment,
some now
the dust devil in the desert

Always Right Behind You

will whirl away into nothingness,
leaving only the vast desert,
only the silent,
unmoving,
undifferentiated
totality of nothingness:
unbeginning
unending
Love.

~ Art

The Problem's Not in the Transmission

Who's to blame when we're unhappy,
dissatisfied,
malcontent?
It starts out being Mom or Dad,
then other kids,
the teacher,
the boss,
him or *her*,
them,
the Universe,
God.

Some of us graduate to the next form
and decide that the problem's within.
So we try to change "ourselves" —
our bodies or our mental characteristics —
in order to get what we think will make us happy.
We may have temporary successes.
The world runs smoother the better we know ourselves.
But it's not sufficient, never enough.
We want lasting peace,
permanent peace of mind,
permanence.

The list of culprits becomes narrower.
We can't expect other people,
themselves impermanent,
to provide us with permanent anything —
much less permanence itself.

So we have to blame the universe,
God,
fate,
whatever put us here.

It's as if we were at the movies,
or at home watching TV,
and we're dissatisfied with the picture,
upset about what's appearing on the screen.
We can blame the producer,
the director,
the cast,
the crew,
the equipment—
or, more generally, the quality and/or content of the transmission
of what's passing through our field of awareness.
Our life sucks, and the problem is in the transmission.

So, what can we do?

We can acquiesce,
accept our fate,
and slide down the drain without protest.

Or we can shake our fist and curse the universe
(or God if we're not staunch believers in No-God).
Or we can cajole God or the Powers-that-Be
if we admit the possibility of such.

Or, if we're a bit more sophisticated,
we can pray the "serenity prayer":
asking for the courage to change the things we can change,
the serenity to accept the things we can't,
and the wisdom to know the difference.

Is There an End?

And what might The Transmitter be telling us
about what we could change
in order to find the lasting fullness we're looking for
if our ears were open?

"Tune the receiver.
The multisensory picture you're getting is picture-perfect.
Every particle and every wave—
every wavicle—
is exactly as it's meant to be
in order to get the message across.
Life is a classroom.
If you apply yourself, you'll get the lesson.
And when you get it, you'll be amazed
beyond your wildest imaginings.
Tune the receiver."

~ Art

Are You a Robot?

There was a poster at the Rose farm[55] with the question: "Are You A Robot?" This, in my opinion, is one of the fundamental questions that all seekers must answer. My initial reaction was "of course not... I am not a robot." It is hard on the ego/self to accept that it may just be a machine. It at once punctures the specialness balloon around our individuality when we start to think about it.

P.D. Ouspensky says man is a machine, but a very peculiar machine. He is a machine, which in the right circumstances and with the right treatment, can know that he is a machine, and having fully realized this, he may find ways to cease to be a machine.

How well do you know yourself? This physical entity that is here, with a certain personality, attributes, dreams, desires, life, mind... whatever is your self-definition at this moment. What about your actions and reactions? Do you control them?

Let's investigate and see how life gets lived. I know several of my friends are addicted to computer games. I have heard that they play for the whole weekend with people from all over the globe. While you are playing the game you get completely sucked into this cyber-reality created by the game generator... you are thinking of strategies, moves, getting your reflexes sharp to attack, defend, jump... or whatever one has to do to play the game. While you are playing, are you aware of how the mind is functioning? Are you different from the character in the game?

---

55 In West Virginia, first home of TAT.

Is There an End?

Isn't this exactly how we go through our lives... do you see the parallel?

G.I. Gurdjieff was of the opinion that unless man makes an effort to remember himself, it is the robot or the machine who sees and experiences life. He asked "Why should we experience so much, only to forget it immediately afterward? Most of our experiences roll off us like a water off a duck's back. Yet the experience is food, with the purpose to enable us to evolve."

Most of the time we are sleepwalking through life. We are on autopilot. Unless something really out of the ordinary is going on, like some sort of emotional turmoil, or you are learning some new skill, or something different from the routine... your attention is wherever.

Life will get spent either way... whether we stay in this state of slumber or make an effort to wake up. Unless you have seen this robotic state that you live in, chances of any change happening are pretty slim. Inner effort towards understanding yourself is required to become human.

G.I. Gurdjieff: "Without self-knowledge, without understanding the working and functions of his machine, man cannot be free, he cannot govern himself and he will always remain a slave."

~ Anima

Seeing What You're Looking Out From

At the last TAT meeting, you discussed the epiphany that occurred when you finally saw what you were looking out from. From your description, it seemed like you saw something that was so obvious (in retrospect) that you don't know how you missed it. You also thought it was akin to Rose's Individual Consciousness of Awareness *on Jacob's Ladder. In the letter I read during the Friday evening session, Bart described it (I think) as follows:*

> "The degree to which you do not exist cannot be overstated. No one has ever become enlightened or Self-realized and no one ever will. No matter how "deep" we look, there is no one.
> "There is, however, what might be called the "ante room" to the Absolute—a realm between, say, no-thought and pure undifferentiated Awareness—where Awareness is somehow witnessing itself as Void. This is as good a description of the "experience" of Self-realization as any. The observer we think we are somehow stumbles into the ante room to the Absolute and "witnesses" No-thing being aware of itself as No-thing, simultaneously realizing that (No-thing being what it is) there is no possibility of there being an observer separate from it."

From my experience in watching the Process Observer... I recall reading the Psychology of the Observer *at the age of 20 and asking myself, "Where am I (my status) on Jacob's Ladder?" Over time, it became quite obvious what Rose meant by* Somatic Awareness, *but its polar opposite—the* Higher Intuition—*was elusive and only became apparent much later in life. Of course, it's crystal clear in retrospect, but by no means did I gain a more accurate perspective during a sudden epiphany.*

Is There an End?

Do you think, for most seekers, that "seeing what you're looking out from" is different than the drawn-out process I encountered as a Process Observer?

When I originally read this letter, my reaction was that I needed to have a better feeling for your mental patterns before I could respond with something that might be helpful. So I asked you some questions that I hoped would give me a better feeling for how to go about undermining your scaffolding:

- What did you see when you watched the process observer? When higher intuition became apparent?
- What did you see when you did the Harding tube experiment?
- What is your current self-definition?

Your silent response reinforces my belief that you're afraid to "duke it out" mentally... afraid of what you'll see... in love with a self-image that you're intuitively aware is a lie. And that "part of you" has the inner child snookered.

I've been watching the 2006 DVD in order to try to spot clips that can be used for our web page. Watched M's presentation and saw what might be an older version of you. He was steady and dynamic as a young guy, but he got scared.

As long as we believe ourselves to be Paul or Art, as long as we're in love with the "I am Paul" or "I am Art" belief, we can't afford to admit what we "see" (intuitively). What occurs when we ask ourselves a question? There's a momentary hiatus as we wait for an answer. During that gap we're aware of what Harding refers to as two-way looking: we're watching the screen where objects of consciousness appear—which you could say is looking outward. But that screen where objects of consciousness appear is Awareness. "What am I?" I'm What's Aware. And what's aware is Self-Aware. Art's not aware of Awareness. Paul's not aware of Awareness. Awareness is Self-Aware.

"Paul" is a system of patterns in the field of observation. I'm saying this to you now, not to Paul, but Heart to Heart: You are always "seeing what you're looking out from"—always have been, always will be.

Originally, I misinterpreted your questions as thought-provokers rather than something meant to obtain more details. So, here's my honest answers to your questions:

- What did you see when you watched the process observer? When higher intuition became apparent?

Whether intuitive or rational, I see thought-forms that are observable entities, distinguishable only in how they arrive in my plane of observation. On one side of the spectrum (somatic awareness), the thoughts pile one on top of another over time until I arrive at what appears to be a logical conclusion. On the other side (intuition), the conclusion is sudden and often occurs with more conviction. Intuitive thoughts seemingly arrive out of nowhere, yet they are often more accurate, especially as I have grown to trust them despite not knowing the reason for the conclusion until sometime later.

- What did you see when you did the Harding tube experiment?

My only experience with the experiment didn't seem productive. I was too bothered by the oddity of staring at someone else in the eye. When all was said and done, I saw a face staring back at me from the end of a white space. That face was not me in any way, shape, or form. No epiphanies or nothing to shake me from my foundation. I would like to try it again with someone I'm more comfortable in working with.

- What is your current self-definition?

Over the past twenty years, the collection of ideas on who I thought I was has dwindled—to the point where I can't identify too much with any daily chores, spiritual books or system, or guru. The only "thing" I see as being my true self is the Observer who witnesses Paul stumble through the day. This observing self is often lost while robot Paul gets caught up in daily exigencies at work and home. I don't know what this observer is, but it will not reveal itself despite an immense frustration, a frustration that is mostly generated by a strong intuition that the picture show called life isn't real.

- M.... was steady and dynamic as a young guy, but he got scared.

This assessment was quite true for me 15 years ago. I wrote (and probably told you) about the time Rose conducted a rapport session in the farmhouse living room at a TAT meeting. He opened the session by hypnotizing several members (including me) and stated that he wanted to duplicate the Jane Slater incident. He was in my head with certainty, and confirmed it by telling me to slow down my thoughts. When I did, he immediately acknowledged aloud the change in my thought patterns. However, I fought him with every fiber of my being. I was scared with what I was about to see and told him so later in the day. I doubt if that would happen today, and here's why: when listening to the recent realizations described by you, Shawn, Bob, Bart, Anima and others, I don't have the fear of losing Paul and being carried out on a stretcher, although I suspect *some type of survival-reaction might kick into gear if my mind thought it was about to die.*

I don't think I'm in love with Paul. I'm immensely frustrated with my inability to figure out why Grace will not descend. When you say "You are always 'seeing what you're looking out from'—always have been, always will be," again I grow frustrated with my inability to grasp this with logic or intuition. I realize that logic and intuition are both products of the mind realm, but alas, nothing has revealed itself to enable me to see with conviction.

I don't know the magic words that will open your eyes, but those "words" exist. That's why the admonition to look under every rock. Bob C. heard them when reading Pulyan; Shawn when reading Merrell-Wolff; Bob F. when reading Bob C. comments to him in the online group. With Rose, it was hearing the "other shoe drop"—seeing that his intended wife's lover was another woman. And so on. If you talk to Shawn, he'll tell you that it wasn't any particular set of words but some overall mood or transmission.

One of the most profound things I ever heard Jim Burns say was that he found he had to let the Light lead him to the Light. Zen master Foyan told his students that they were always in the Light but that they didn't see it even with their eyes open. Same goes for you and Grace.

You say "I'm immensely frustrated with my inability to figure out why Grace will not descend." Any word beginning with a capital letter, like Grace, points to what you really are, your identity, not some remote Other in contrast to a local self. All thoughts are God's. Paul is a thought. The quoted statement is a thought that Awareness has projected onto Itself (the screen of Awareness). Consider that Awareness seemingly splits into subject and objects in order to know itself. One of those objects is the thought: "I'm immensely frustrated in my ability to figure out why Grace will not descend."

Good! Frustration should produce action. But there's something preventing action in your case I think, something short-circuiting action. Do you have any idea what it is? There's some fear or pride that's maintaining the status quo, allowing you to continue not seeing something that a part of you doesn't want to see. What aren't you willing to let go of? (I'm referring to a belief, not to something material.) If it's not the fear side of the coin that seems to be up, then it's pride.

"I grow frustrated with my inability to grasp this with logic or intuition"—when I add that to the other frustration statement, I get the picture of Paul insisting that God come to him. In other words, Paul wants to expand to encompass God. That's not the way it works. Paul has to go to God. (Remember Mr. Rose saying that the student had to get himself to the edge of the abyss before effective transmission could occur? Before that, the seeker would have no way of knowing whether the view was real or imaginary.) This going generally takes the form of fighting or struggle, but it always ends in surrender, letting go. Paul is not going to grasp God. There will come a time when Paul will become zero. If circumstances are right when that occurs, then "Paul" will know what he really is.

"Nothing has revealed itself to enable me to see with conviction"—that's only due to one reason, which is a faulty belief about that "me." Awareness has a hypnotic focus on "I am Paul." The individual is like a closed fist. Life gradually weakens the clenched muscles, allowing or forcing them to relax, and the fist opens. This fist is clamped onto a faulty belief about the self. When it eventually opens, what it has been grasping is seen to be a concept without substance.

"This observing self is often lost while robot Paul gets caught up in daily exigencies"—the observing self (Awareness) has never been lost.

"My true self is the Observer"—the Observer is not a self in the sense that you conceive self. The term is misleading. It's an Empty Observatory that is aware. There's no attendant in the Lighthouse.

> AT: What are you?
> PC: I'm the Observer.
> AT: Are you what's aware?
> PC: Yes.
> AT: How do you know that?
> PC: Because I'm aware of Awareness.
> AT: Isn't Awareness what's aware?
> PC: Yes, sure.
> AT: Do you see a contradiction here?
> PC: Well....
> AT: Are there two Awarenesses?

If each person's real identity is What's Aware, how many awarenesses are in the room when you and your wife are together? When you are at a TAT meeting? When two people have their heads in a Harding tube? On the Penn State campus at State College?

If you flip the frustration coin over, what's on the longing side? Frustration is the push, longing the pull. Do you communicate with your inner self? Do you put your glimpses and longing into words—interior monologue, exterior journaling? (Forms of prayer.)

Have you evaluated where things stand for you on the threefold path recently?

Have you identified your deepest desire? Accepted it as your #1 priority? Become a vector toward it?

Is There an End?

Have you accepted your Lord and announced in your heart the desire to surrender to the Lord in thought, word and deed?

Have you asked your real self, your Lord, for help? Do you look/listen for His response? Does your inner self try to communicate in dreams?

Have you become an adult who no longer is aware of the inner Child? What appeals to you? Mike C. was struck by the "Woodcutter" poem in a recent Forum and acted on his inspiration by getting the Samuel books. There's magic throughout manifestation. Manifestation itself is magic. When the fist opens, the appearance of becoming occurs.

❦

The above correspondence occurred in November-December 2006. Paul had a breakthrough the following May. See the downloads section of www.searchwithin.org for an account of what occurred.

~ Art

7

Colors of Love

Falling in Love

Over the past month or so, I fell in love with this girl and we became very close, very fast. We crossed the chasms from strangers to being close by being completely honest with each other, taking off our "masks." But at some point, I realized that we could never cross the final chasm between us. That we could never be one. This was one of the greatest pains I've ever felt. Because it's the one thing I want more than anything else, and I was forced to see that it could never be.

I remember you talking about the pain of being a separate individual, and I guess I should finish your book [Solid Ground of Being], but I don't remember you talking about how you ever overcame it. I mean, I know it's all the same pursuit, but from this angle? I guess in recent months, I've been driven to be more open and honest with the people in my life. To not hide things. To not try so hard to protect my self-image. I wish I could break down the walls between us, but everything, in the grand scheme of things, seems futile. Is there anything you found valuable along these lines? To be honest, I don't know how you could possibly answer this email. But I just felt like I couldn't not ask for help.

How we overcome the limitation is really simple—we just keep looking for unconditional love, for the state of being beyond separation. It's a progression of disillusionments, of seeing through faulty self-beliefs until we hit the final one. Since we fail into final success, any specific advice would have to be wrong advice in order to work. The only foolproof advice is to persevere.

What's futile is finding no-separation in this dimension of separation (i.e., the mind and cosmos). We have to return to our source… recognizing the simple fact of what we truly *are… to find what we long for. And what we're looking for is, truly, closer than close. The flower bud struggles to open to find the warmth of the sun, the seed struggles to burst open to find the love of its source. It seems so poignant from down here. But what created the blossom, the seed, the man, the woman, etc., has never been separate from them. It has been dreaming a dream of separation through its creation.*

※

The friend who wrote the italicized paragraphs above is a young man who astutely recognized that the pain of separation could never be solved by personal love, no matter how profound. Even when we experience the rapport of "one mind" with another person, it's evanescent. Personal love cannot answer the deep longing for unconditional, unlimited love that ends the angst of believing we are a separate, vulnerable being.

~ Art

Sahajo Bai

Sahajo Bai was a Rajput princess in the 18th century. On her wedding day, when she was being dressed, Sant Charandas (a renowned Delhi guru) showed up and asked if she was going to spend her life in some momentary marital bliss or would try finding something Permanent. These words were enough for Sahajo to leave her home on her wedding day and follow her Guru on the quest to find eternal bliss. The story goes that through her devotion and determination, she found Eternal Love

She expresses her devotion and gratitude toward her guru in these verses:

> I can leave Ram[56] but not guru
> I don't want to look at Hari[57] when my guru is there
> Hari got me into this world and
> Guru got me out of this coming and going
> Hari gave me the five thieves (5 senses)
> Guru got this orphan rid of these addictions
> Hari got me into this family/relationship web
> Guru cut off all my attachments
> Hari got me entangled in all these ailments and appetites
> Guru made me into a sannyasin to get rid of all
> Hari got me into this cycle of karma and maya
> Guru introduced me to mySelf
> Hari hid himself from me

---

56 Ram(achandra): One of the most widely worshipped Hindu deities, the embodiment of chivalry and virtue.
57 Hari: a name for the supreme absolute in the Vedas. Hari refers to God who takes away all the sorrows of his devotees.

Guru lighted the lamp for me
then Hari got me into this struggle for Freedom
but Guru removed all the illusions

I give my heart and soul to Charandas
Hari I can leave, but not my guru…

Sahajo Bai must have been a real kindred spirit, a brave girl. Walking out with her Guru on her wedding day, coming from a conservative society, couldn't have been easy. She must have had complete faith in her Guru that he would help her in reaching the final destination. She must have been a teenager, as girls were married off early during that time period. It makes me wonder how she even realized that inner longing at that young age.

~ Anima

Mr. Wetherill

*M*esa Verde was the home of pueblo dwellers from about 600 to 1300 AD. Dayton Duncan and Ken Burns, in *The National Parks*,[58] tell about its modern discovery:

> A few months before Rudyard Kipling visited Yellowstone, some cowboys searching for stray cattle in southwestern Colorado, along the edge of a high plateau known as Mesa Verde, came upon what looked to them like the ruins of an ancient city, with buildings three stories high, tucked into the side of a cliff. Using a tree trunk and their lariats, they improvised a ladder and descended for a closer look. "Things were arranged in the rooms," one of them recalled, "as if people might just have been out visiting somewhere."

The cowboys who chanced on the cliff dwellings in 1889 were the five Wetherill brothers from a Quaker family that had moved to the area from Kansas eight years earlier and were grazing cattle on land of friendly Utes around the mesa.

One of the brothers, Richard, wanted to become a respected archaeologist and formed an expedition to search the Southwest for other ruins. He discovered the Kiet Siel pueblo ruins in northeastern Arizona and located remains in southeastern Utah of a basket-making culture that predated the pueblo Anasazi.

Another Quaker family from Kansas, the Palmers, were talented musicians who toured the U.S. The father, Sidney, had heard about a pueblo ruin at Chaco Canyon in northeastern

---

58 *The National Parks: America's Best Idea* is the companion volume to the twelve-hour PBS series.

New Mexico, and the family accompanied Richard Wetherill there. Wetherill fell in love with the Palmers' 19-year-old daughter, Marietta, they married in 1896, and in 1898 they settled near the impressive Pueblo Bonito in Chaco Canyon.

About ten years later, a new Indian agent among the Navajos apparently became jealous of Wetherill's ties with the Chaco Canyon Indians and told them that Wetherill's cattle business would push their sheep off all the grazing land. One of the Navajos shot and killed Wetherill in 1910. Marietta later wrote:

> Less than a year after Mr. Wetherill died I moved from Pueblo Bonito... I was a gypsy the rest of my life... Chaco Canyon still haunted me.
> I want... the world [to] give Mr. Wetherill credit for what he did... and the sort of person he was.
> I will tell you this: if we could put the time back and I was a girl again, there is no man I would want to marry but Mr. Wetherill.

~ Art

What Do I Know of Love?

Falling in love is not something we do
But is being taken over by something other.
Temporarily the image of self recedes
And the image of an other takes center stage
Standing in the floodlight of adoration.
First love is most shocking perhaps
Giving us the first taste
        of the solution to the problem
                of life and death.
When we fall in love we surrender
The preeminence of self.

~ Art

Uninvited Guest

Love, O Love, you hurt a lot.
How did you find me? I was hiding all along.
I didn't want you or invite you into my heart
but you sneaked up and now you are all around,
inside, outside,
in this and that...

You make me wonder
how did I ever miss you or not know you
couldn't recognize you maybe...
buried deep under the business of my heart.

Don't you have something else to do?
How can you stand and smile now,
while causing so much confusion and pain.
Are you here to prove to me
that that there is no solace,
this pain of separation will not go away.

Is there any going back once you are realized...[59]
Is this intense yearning really You?
Love, O Love, please go away
And find someone else to play your game...

~ Anima

---

59 Pre-realization speculation.

Futility of Love?

A friend wrote the following in response to the double question: "What was a sharp affliction to your sense of self? How did your mind attempt to recover from the hit?"

Having my friendships/love rejected (feeling I love someone more than he/she loves me and feeling ridiculed for feeling and expressing love). The feeling of being rejected and unloved came to me repeatedly without enough counter-feeling over the course of my youth, up to the point that I made a vow to not love, or at least, express love to friends anymore. I developed a sense of apathy combined with a sense of loneliness, abandonment, and constant battle with the world. Up to this day I am attempting to recover by trying to live and plan a life in which I can be as much independent from people as I can be. Another affliction comes in the form of conviction that the attempt is futile, that is, I see that despite my great doubt of the possibility, I still want love, a sincere one. It leads to constant tension and anxiety in the background, and feeling worn-out.

Your response confirms what I've felt about you since I've gotten to know you. I think now that you've communicated it, I may be able to help you a little more.

Everyone is looking for love, and life holds a variety of disappointments for love-seekers... sometimes in major shocks, sometimes lesser shocks spread over a long period.

We can't conceive of the absolute Love that we're looking for, so the mind latches onto a particular form of love that holds out the hope of providing satisfaction of the longing. If the world withholds the type of love the mind conceives of, we make up a story about being unworthy, unappreciated, etc. Either way it elevates the ego. If the world provides what we think will satisfy the longing and it turns out not to be the absolute love we're looking for, we may decide that the specifics weren't right and begin looking again for the same type of love. Then, or eventually, we may realize that no instance of what we conceive of is going to provide the permanent, total love we want.

Our reaction may be a conviction of futility and resulting depression, or if we're fortunate, something may awaken the intuition that the total love we're looking for is possible even if not conceivable. Intuition tells us that "outside" is constant change and impermanence and that what we're looking for can only be found within. That will set up a new dynamic, where we're still hoping for a temporary, conceivable solution and yet we know, deep down, we'll never be satisfied until/unless we find a total, permanent solution.

~ Art

Capacity to Love

Our capacity to love expands
as our view expands;
our view expands
as we realize what we're not.

We can't love fully
while we feel vulnerable;
we feel vulnerable
while we're a thing apart.

We get a taste of love
for our defenseless babies,
and as children
for our impeccable parents.

Yet it's not true love,
for it doesn't last;
true love
has never abandoned us.

And never will.

~ Art

Peace Prayer of St. Francis of Assisi

Lord, make me an instrument of your peace;
where there is hatred, let me sow love;
where there is injury, pardon;
where there is doubt, faith;
where there is despair, hope;
where there is darkness, light;
and where there is sadness, joy.

Grant that I may not so much seek
to be consoled as to console;
to be understood
as to understand;
to be loved as to love;
for it is in giving
that we receive,
it is in pardoning
that we are pardoned.
And it is in dying
that we are born to eternal life.

Feelings About Love

*P*articipants in a men's self-inquiry retreat recorded these feelings about love:

Did love pass me by
Or does it hide in plain sight

Does its lack fuel my search for Truth
Do I simply long for a loving mother's touch

How will I know Love when I see it.

Will I feel its warm embrace
But must I first give to then receive it
Must I trim repression's claws
Or will love itself heal me, asking nothing in return.

Love may be the answer
Identity may be its form
A will equal B
And all will be as one.

But... no "buts" will be accepted
Somehow all will be included
When the mind and heart are united
And are free to soar as one.

❦

Love is the rain a full cloud dumps on everything below. Love is the mother feeding the child from the breast. Love is the father firmly guiding his son. Love is my heart and the desire to be. Love is what's entered my heart and begun to heal. Love is two brothers helping one another. Love is giving freely and receiving freely. Love is what keeps me here and what is beckoning me home. Love is the field of daffodils that turned to watch me as I went by. Love is the snow that sparkled back at me with ten thousand infinite sparkles as I flew above. Love is my heart. Love is forgiveness, and asking forgiveness. Love is completion & returning home from whence I came.

*

Love leaves roses
    in the overlooked corners
of a wind-spun story.
A pedal floats on the
    soft sounds of a
    dying man's eased breath
A red bloom brightens the
face of a weary friend
tired in grief.
And where is this Love
who stirs the heart's
desperate grasp,
Leaving bittersweet reminders
    of the holy presence
    just departed?
This Love was known
    in some vague past,

but left rejected
by the pride of me.
I scorned Love's trust
and let Love go,
choosing instead
to embrace my self.
But Love's here, Love's here,
ever so close.
The sweet fragrance
of Home's warm embrace
still haunts the room.

What are my feelings about love?
1. Want, want, want
2. Always comes with a price
3. Always incomplete and unsatisfying
4. Anger at #2 and #3
5. Missing; possibly what's missing
6. Unsafe to give
7. Bitterness at #6
8. A weakness that loveless others can take advantage of
9. Not in my future
10. Probably always available but resisted
11. A potential source of feeling secure

12. Hopefully part of my future
13. Not really from other people
14. Potentially contradictory of my identity
15. Disgusting, though, when mixed with fear
16. More valuable than material wealth
17. No sadness, interestingly

※

*I don't want to seem
childish. My first reaction to the word
I can only catch sideways*

*but after the word, the feeling, the positive
projection of my longing, the other
end of the cord that extends from my heart, directly.*

※

I recently had a chance to closely observe pure parental love being bestowed on a young child. What I came away with was seeing how love is the life-giving, life-sustaining warmth that runs the universe.

Despite this, love is something I look away from. For love to exist, there has to be an "other." This "other" must be capable of unconditional love, must be infallible, and permanent. It must also have my interests as its top priority. Based on current evidence, it seems ridiculous to base my desires and cravings on the existence of such an entity. It's best to try to squelch and look away from any desire I have for it.

And yet, there's the feeling that if I could catch one glimpse of this Divine Love, I would do all I can to go towards it. How long do I have to wait?

Love is unbearably beautiful and
I long to lose myself in Love.

Pursuit of Relentless Love

I am pursuing you with relentless love,
awaiting your return with infinite patience,
ready to enfold you in the boundless love of true identity.

When you've suffered long enough
with your dreams of temporal satisfaction,
turn around and come home.

I am always waiting to guide you
since I know you've lost your way.
I am always right behind you.

~ Art

Bhagwan's Love: Man & Desire

One day Bhagwan[60] was idling away. With nothing better to do, He started wondering how his creation was unfolding. He thought He should test his systems and laws, see if everything is working the way it is meant to be. He was also curious to see if His favorite creation, man, would outwit His laws that holds the universe together.

He looked around and found his strongest, best creation, a sage, Purushottam,[61] who had made his life a prayer, an inspiration to the rest. The sage had lived his life from his highest state of being, where his dharma and his inner values were the way of his life. Temptations couldn't touch him. He lived the highest ideals, the purest state, the strongest man, the most beautiful that Bhagwan becomes. He was Love.

Dusht[62] Bhagwan, just out of sheer mischievousness, planted a little desire on the way of Sage Purushottam's walk. The strong sage, unaware of Bhawan's game, tripped over it one morning while out for his walk. And before he knew it, he noticed his heart was consumed by this intense fire for the other which wouldn't let him rest. The sage found himself to be desperate. He had to find a way to satisfy these inner urges. He couldn't think anymore. He who had loved Truth his entire life started lying not only to others but to himself to justify his desperate actions. The actions, which he knew pretty well, were devaluing the inner self that he was scared of losing. Fear controlled his life now. One who didn't know fear previously started acting like a coward. He was enslaved

---

60 Hindi word for God, the Creator.
61 Perfect/best man.
62 Hindi word for troublemaker.

by a little desire. He couldn't think or see straight. His eyes were filled with tears over his broken, unfulfilled dream.

Love was trying to acquire love...

Bhagwan was very pleased to see that everything was operating in PERFECTION. Desire was perfect, the mortal was perfect, laws were working, everything was in accordance with how He needed it to be. The sun would keep burning and the earth spinning, and He could rest. "Man is not above my laws yet," thought the Creator.

"But why does my heart feel heavy?" Bhagwan wondered.

~ Anima

Stumbling into Love

This story begins in Pakistan in 1993, the year I attempted to climb K2, the world's second-highest mountain, only to be forced to turn back two thousand feet shy of the summit. After making my way back to K2 base camp, I then got lost while trekking down the thirty-nine-mile Baltoro Glacier and wound up staggering into a little village called Korphe (pronounced "KOR-fay"), a place so destitute that one in every three children perished before the age of one. It was in Korphe that I was provided with shelter, food, tea, and a bed. And it was in Korphe one afternoon during my recuperation that I stumbled across eighty-two children sitting outside writing their lessons with sticks in the dirt, with no teacher in sight. One of those students was a girl named Chocho, and somehow she got me to promise the community that I would someday return and build them a school.

The fulfillment of that promise involves a tale that recounts my fumbling efforts in Berkeley, where I worked as a nurse, to sell my car, my climbing gear, and all of my books in order to raise the necessary money—and the subsequent chain of events through which a lost mountaineer eventually came to discover his life's calling by fostering education and literacy in the impoverished Muslim villages of the western Himalayas.

The preceding excerpt comes from Greg Mortenson's introduction to his book titled *Stones into Schools: Promoting Peace with Books, not Bombs, in Afghanistan and Pakistan*. At the writing of this second book, the nonprofit institute he founded had established more than 130 schools in the remotest areas of those two countries. *Stones into Schools* is a true adventure story, beautifully written, of Greg's 1999 promise to a group of Kirghiz horsemen—descendants of nomadic tribes from the Tuva region of Siberia who had settled in the Pamir highlands, a remote edge of civilization at the eastern edge of a corridor between the Pamir and Karakoram ranges, where Afghanistan touches China—and the resulting actions.

The horsemen had ridden for six days without stopping, sent as emissaries by their *khan*, who'd gotten word that Greg was in the Hindu Kush across the Irshad Pass connecting the Wakhan Corridor of Afghanistan to the northern edge of Pakistan.

Permission to accomplish anything in the Wakhan Corridor required the agreement of the leaders of three diverse groups, and access for supplies, which had to come in on the one road through the corridor—the section of the old Silk Road running from Yazd, Iran to Kashgar, China—was controlled by the westernmost of the three khans. And his permission depended on building a school for him first.

The required school for the Tajik khan was completed in May of 2004, just as a series of riots set off by a rumor, later proved untrue, of a guard at the Guantánamo prison flushing a copy of the *Koran* down a toilet, led Greg to a shelter under protection of the Tajik khan that was being shared with other travelers. One of those travelers turned out to be the Kirghiz khan, who was returning empty-handed from a trip to Kabul to plead with Hamid Karzai for help.

Describing their meeting and the drafting of an agreement to build a school with the Kirghiz of the Little Pamir, Mortenson wrote: "Thus ended one of the most memorable encounters I have experienced during the twelve years since I failed to climb K2 and wound up stumbling into the village of Korphe." And that's only a third of the way into the book.

~ Art

Giridhar Is My True Love

I am going to Giridhar's house;
Giridhar[63] is my true Love.
My heart is smitten by his looks
I wake up when it is still night
I come as soon as it is dawn.
Night and day I play with him,
By this and that I woo him.
Wherever he wants me to sit, I sit;
If he sells me, I'll get sold.
His and my love story is old;
Every second I live for him.
Whatever he wants me to wear, I wear;
Whatever he gives, I eat.
Meera's[64] prabhu[65] is Giridhar Naagar;
Again and again I die for him.

The story of Meera Bai, an Indian saint:[66]

Meera was born to a Rajput ruler, Rana Ratansingh of Kurkhi in Mewad district of Rajasthan. The year was 1547 A.D. These were times of intense fighting between the Mughals and Rajput rulers. She was expected to learn the ways of Rajput princesses. In time, she would be married off to a prince, and was expected to move from behind one curtain (purdah) to another. Only a society which has been subjected to the ruthlessness of invading forces can understand the resulting fear. The Rajputs gave two reasons for their fierce pride: their

---

63 Giridhar is a name for Krishna
64 Meera Bai, the singer of this bhajan, translated by Anima from Hindi.
65 Lord
66 From the Bhakti List Archives, www.ramanuja.org

men's valour and the women's strict adherence to their behavior code. These were non-negotiables.

For some inexplicable reason, the Lord chose this setting for Meera.

A sannyasi[67] visited the palace, and the child Meera was completely fascinated with the idol of Lord Krishna that he carried. She begged until he gave the idol to her. Later, watching a marriage procession, the little girl asked her mother who her own bride-groom was, and the Lord made her mother speak those prophetic words: "Do you see this idol of Giridhar Gopal? He is your husband...."

Meera grew up, getting more and more attached to her Lord. But as per custom, when the time came, she was married off to prince Bhoja, son of Maharana Pratap. (Those who remember school history lessons may recognize the name as one famous for bravery in wars against the Mughals.) One can only imagine how detached Meera felt in that milieu and how abnormal they thought she was. Her in-laws' family deity was Goddess Durga, but Meera refused to pray to anyone but her Krishna. At first the prince wanted to humour her, and he built a temple within the palace for her Lord Sri Krishna. She would spend hours there, dancing and singing....

Soon the public began to take notice, and large throngs of men and women would appear at the temple to join in the dancing and singing. Prince Bhoja withstood the jealous rumours this caused, and Meera's fervour increased day by day....

It is said that when the Emperor Akbar too heard of her and visited the temple in disguise with his court musician Tansen, the prince could take it no more. He asked Meera to go drown in the river rather than bring

---

67 A religious ascetic who has renounced the world by performing his own funeral and abandoning all claims to social or family standing.

further shame to the royal family. Meera went to do his bidding when she felt someone hold her back. It was her dear Lord Krishna, who asked her to go to Brindavan and wait for Him....

Meera Bai

Love's Response[68]

Darling,
My heart,
Through you I feel.
When you feel me partially,
You feel separation.
When you feel me completely,
You are complete...
You *are* me.
Feeling me partially,
You are human,
I am you,
And I feel the struggle of my children
To find me.
When you feel me partially,
You reach out to another
Of your brothers and sisters
For personal consolation.
But when you remember me,
You remember that your higher calling
Is to help your others
Find their way home to me.
Love's sacrifice
Becomes Love's reward.

~ Art

---

68   To "Uninvited Guest" above in this chapter.

8

Tales, East & West

Profound Writings, East & West

Richard Rose's book with the above title is a brilliant selection of excerpts from esoteric and philosophic writings classical and more recent, organized into the following sections:

- Ramana Maharshi Excerpts
- The Book of the Golden Precepts
- The Poetry of Francis Thompson
- Elegant Sayings
- Excerpts from the Himalayas of the Soul
- Three Books of the Absolute
- The Lecture of Questions
- Excerpt from the *Bhagavad Gita*
- Wisdom of Franz Hartmann

An example, from the *Isa Upanishad*:

> He moves, and He moves not. He is far, and He is near. He is within all, and He is outside all.
>
> When a sage sees this great Unity and his Self has become all beings, what delusion and what sorrow can ever be near him?
>
> Into deep darkness fall those who follow action. Into deeper darkness fall those who follow knowledge.

One is the outcome of knowledge, and another is the outcome of action. Thus have we heard from the ancient sages who explained this truth to us.

He who knows both knowledge and action, with action overcomes death and with knowledge reaches immortality.

Into deep darkness fall those who follow the immanent. Into deeper darkness fall those who follow the transcendent.[69]

---

69 Footnote by Richard Rose:
   Who follow the immanent—means those who retreat into the luxury of imagination, believing they can create objects of desire, by physical means.
   Who follow the transcendent—means those who try to *objectify* transcendent possibilities or possible attainments, rather than wait to realize transcendent powers or truths.

Rose ends the book with an untitled poem, which begins:

> I come to you as a man selling air,
> And you will think twice at the offer and price,
> And you will argue that nothing is there,
> Although we know that it is—everywhere.[70]

~ Art

---

[70] See the complete poem in the *TAT Forum* archive (https://tatfoundation.org/forum2017-12.htm#6).

Hey, Girlfriend!

*H*ave you ever wondered why you hear of more men who are awake than women?

I had read some religious text that to be Enlightened, you have to be born as a male. If you look, there are not many women you will find who are enlightened compared to men. So what happens to a woman who feels that she wants nothing more from life than Liberation? Is there any chance for her to make it? Our limitations come from whatever we identify with. For example, if I am the house, then I am unable to move. If I am my body-mind, then I exist in time and space; I am born and will die; I am a separate individual, driven by my instincts, desires and fears.

This is not about gender equality or superior/inferior sexes but investigating if there are significant and meaningful differences that pave the path of how women seek. And if that makes a difference in reaching our goal of Self-Realization.

Are male and female brains wired differently?

The British team of geneticist Anne Moir and science journalist David Jessel looked at how sex difference is apparent in the unmistakable brain and neural wiring of the human being.[71] According to them, there is a male and a female brain just as sure as there is male and female genitalia. Scientists can easily determine a person's sex with a brain scan. Based on their own work and that of others, Moir and Jessel explain with equal parts boldness, clarity, and sureness:

> ... The truth is that virtually every professional scientist and researcher into the subject has concluded that the

---

[71] *Brain Sex: The Real Difference Between Men and Women*

brains of men and women are different... The nature and cause of brain differences are now known beyond speculation, beyond prejudice, and beyond a reasonable doubt... There has seldom been a greater divide between what intelligent, enlightened opinion presumes— that men and women have the same brain—and what sciences know—that they do not.

What role does Nature play in our Awakening?

How our life unfolds is governed by biology and sociology. It became a big concern for me when I thought about my chances of finding an end to my suffering. The thought of continuing on the same trajectory of life was in itself the most depressing thought. But then it occurred to me: "To whom does it make a difference that I am a woman or a man?" Is the Absolute setting up any criteria and yardstick about who will measure up and get to the end? Who is deciding this end?

But then on this path of "Know Thyself" can we bypass the work of knowing how our physiology affects our thinking and our actions? What are the underlying beliefs about our strengths and weaknesses that may or may not be hindering the chances of reaching our goal?

Are there gender-distinct differences across diverse cultures that affect a woman's path as a seeker? Here are some of my very basic observations that I found to be different in male and female psychology that might influence how the two genders seek.

Women draw their identity from their relationships, whereas man defines himself with what he does. I think nature has programmed women to ensure the continuation of the species. There is a native American saying that when a child cries, the man goes out to hunt and the woman runs to check on the child. Her children, and then the world, are almost an extension of her. The woman is much more deeply rooted in her nest and her world. She is more invested in the creation. If creation is nothing but Maya, then she is completely sucked into this Maya, the illusion. To objectify it and to say Not-This, Not-This can't be easy. This, in my opinion, is the major obstacle, her inability to see her identification with her attachments.

Man's mind is very sequential and logical. Sharad, my husband, would help me debug the computer programs that I would find extremely frustrating to deal with. He seemed to enjoy it, whereas it used to be sheer torture for me. Detailed and tedious tasks kill me. As women, we are quite attached to our spontaneity. For me to be able to question myself or anyone else does not come easily. I like to be agreeable for the most part (this is my self-image). Questioning for me is really an acquired skill but one of the most essential on this path of Self-Inquiry. How can there be any inquiry if you have inner resistance to 'inquiry'? And the caveat is that you cannot fake it. It cannot be superficial but has to come from your cells, with conviction.

Women for sure have a much higher EQ than men. It's not good to generalize, but this is my personal observation. This can become a major hurdle because we thrive on emotions and feelings. Everything is measured with the yardstick of our feelings. Once I started to observe my emotions, I realized how fickle and transitory emotions are. It seemed mine changed on a second-to-second basis. How do you trust all your actions and reactions to life based on your emotions? I don't think I ever managed to control my emotions or my actions. The emotional crests and troughs did flatten out a little bit when observed, where at least I felt my mind stabilized a little more comparatively. Now here is an interesting fact I discovered: ALL thinking has emotion at its base.

Going through the menstrual cycle leads to fluctuating moods influenced by hormones. Finding consistency in your behavior/actions can become a big challenge when your hormones are changing and affecting the color of your glasses, which is your mood. No wonder Mr. Rose said that women have the best chance of waking up before puberty hits or after menopause. Also having children is a huge energy/attention expenditure. But then this experience of going through pregnancy and motherhood helps ripen the fruit faster.

One big difference that I found in male and female psychology is a woman's willingness to surrender. Though surrender in itself is another tough concept to ponder over and is quite hard to grasp, it can be the shortest and most direct path to God. Just surrender without any ifs and buts. It is much easier for a woman to see through her ego, that is if it gets her attention. She gets sidetracked in worshiping the gods/deities/authority, or in nurturing her nest. Her existential angst originates from the suffering she feels from the separation from her Source. For a woman it is not about her identity, who she is, but finding completion. Unless she learns to discern, she keeps looking for completion in the world… in relationships, creativity, practices, teachers. As a woman, I felt it was easy for me to forget my original goal and get busy with the scenery. Whereas man, once determined, can get laser focused.

Man's Achilles heel is his 'pride' in his individuality. He would rather kill himself then let anyone know of his vulnerabilities. The question that propels the man is the "Who am I?" question. Unlike a woman, he tries his best to avoid feeling his feelings. He would rather rationalize his emotions than feel them. Resistance only increases suffering.

Somewhere along the way, the seeker gets wise and embraces both her feminine and masculine sides. Intuition, feelings, rational mind, intellect... all are used towards one goal of finding a permanent end to all your suffering or whatever your heart desires.

※

The path of love and the path of knowledge cannot remain separate.

~ Anima

Svetaketu

Here is a conversation between student and teacher[72] where the student is eager to learn and the teacher is willing to teach That which cannot be taught....

> When Svetaketu was twelve years old, he was sent to a teacher with whom he studied until he was twenty-four. After learning all the Vedas, he returned home full of conceit and pride in the belief that he was consummately well-educated and very censorious.
>
> His father said to him, "Svetaketu, my child, you are so full of your learning and so censorious, have you asked for that knowledge by which we hear the unhearable, by which we perceive what cannot be perceived and know what cannot be known?"
>
> "What is that knowledge, sir?" asked Svetaketu.
>
> His father replied, "As by knowing one lump of clay all that is made of clay is known—so, my child, is that knowledge, knowing which we know all."
>
> "But surely these venerable teachers of mine are ignorant of this knowledge; for if they possessed it they would have imparted it to me. Do you, sir, therefore, give me that knowledge?"
>
> "So be it," said the father. And he said, "Bring me a fruit of the Nyagrodha[73] tree."

---

72 From the *Chandogya Upanishad*
73 Banyan (Ficus benghalensis)

"Here it is, sir."

"Break it."

"It is broken, sir."

"What do you see there?"

"Some seeds, sir, exceedingly small."

"Break one of these."

"It is broken, sir."

"What do you see there?"

"Nothing at all."

The father said, "My son, that subtle essence which you do not perceive there—in that very essence stands the being of the huge Nyagrodha tree. In that which is the subtle essence of all that exists has its self. That is the True, that is the Self, and thou Svetaketu art That."

"Pray, sir", said the son, "tell me more."

"Be it so, my child", the father replied; and he said, "Place this salt in water, and come to me tomorrow morning."

The son did as he was told.

Next morning the father said, "Bring me the salt you put in the water."

The son looked for it, but could not find it, for the salt, of course, had dissolved.

The father said, "Taste some of the water from the surface of the vessel. How is it?"

"Salty."

"Taste some from the middle. How is it?"

"Salty."

"Taste some from the bottom. How is it?"

"Salty."

The father said, "Throw the water away and then come back to me again."

The son did so; but the salt was not lost, for the salt existed forever.

Then the father said, "Here likewise in this body of yours, my son, you do not perceive the True; but there, in fact, it is. In that which is the subtle essence, all that exists has its self. That is the True, that is the Self, and thou, Svetaketu, art That."

This story makes you realize how attention is always drawn to the pots and pans and never to the Clay out of which the shapes emerge. Even when the shapes are destroyed, Clay remains. Can a pot come into existence without the Clay. Does Clay need the pot to be what it is? How can this pot, Anima, turn its attention towards the Clay that it is made of?

Where is that latent Life which makes the seed turn into this huge tree?

Can salty water realize its saltiness?

Can pot, seed, or water know the subtle Source from their present state of existence?

The Guru has the love and patience for his student, like a father has for his son, to give him the Knowledge that is above and beyond any knowledge that the student could get from the world of the pot. He gets to know That which is the Source of him and all.

~ Anima

The Paradox of Acceptance

A friend has suffered recurring bouts of clinical depression for about 10 years, since his second year in grad school. He doesn't think of his state of mind as having a conviction of hopelessness, but the symptoms include panic, uncontrolled worry about making mistakes, uncontrolled crying, inability to make decisions, and feeling like people in his life would be better off without him.

I suffered through seven years of undiagnosed depression triggered by a conviction that what I wanted most from life was hopeless for me. What broke my depression was an acceptance experience that occurred when on a solitary retreat.

Shortly before that retreat, I had retrieved a book by Hubert Benoit[74] off my bookshelf, which I had read maybe 15 years earlier but didn't "get." And leafing through the book—unusual for me—I came across his definition of acceptance: Unlike resignation, acceptance follows from "considering something with our whole being and arriving at the view that we wouldn't change it even if we had the power to do so." And my mind immediately started arguing with the idea. Acceptance would cast all the things I didn't like about myself into concrete—or worse, into Lucite, where others could see them.

At the beginning of the retreat, I found myself making a list of maybe a dozen "pain balloons" I'd carried around with me for years—mainly situations where I had felt embarrassed or diminished in some way. And I saw myself pick a random item from the list and then watch the mind

---

74 *The Supreme Doctrine: Psychological Studies in Zen Thought*

go into a previously-unseen turbo-drive mode of processing an amazing amount of information way more rapidly than I could see more than bits and pieces of, processing the question of whether I could accept that situation in Benoit's terms—that is, deciding not to change it if I had the power to change it.

After maybe 20 minutes, the process came to a quiet conclusion: I don't have a big enough "computer" to change something in the past without the possibility of things turning out drastically worse than they had. I then watched myself select another item from the list, again going into the turbo-drive mode, processing a new set of information from the database of my life experience... and after a similar amount of time, again coming up with the same conclusion.

What followed was the sensation of going upward, although I was still conscious of my body sitting in a chair, and getting an instantaneous new view. My mind described the new view in these terms: From up here, everything down there is perfect just as it was and is.

One of the things that shocked me was that I could accept things about myself as they had been and were now without having to like them. And I found, subsequently, that rather than acceptance preventing change, it actually loosened things up to where change could occur.

Acceptance doesn't imply resignation. But it takes the focus off the symptoms (whether we're feeling hopeful or hopeless about changing them), off the reaction of suffering from them, and allows us to focus on the BIG problem of life and death, and on the search for our true identity or completion.

~ Art

Going Home

I've been reading through the AA big book and found it surprisingly inspiring despite my hang-ups with higher powers. It hit me the other day that I was basically projecting my idea of God onto the term "higher power" and then rejecting that. When looking at just the simple question of "Is there a power greater than myself?" the obvious intellectual (and occasionally emotional) answer is yes. Despite that, however, there's a big block in opening up to this sense of a power greater than myself, and many rationalizations going on about my own control... even the cliché "I'm in control 'cause I can stop when I want."

Did you ever go through the steps around the time that you were going to AA meetings? I remember you saying you only found yourself praying when really backed into a corner and was curious how this affected your view of the 12 steps. That first step is a doozy.

Here's what I remember of working the 12-step program (going to meetings and working with a sponsor in the mid-1990s):

1. We admitted we were powerless over alcohol—that our lives had become unmanageable.

- I believed that I was powerless and my life had become unmanageable.

2. Came to believe that a Power greater than ourselves could restore us to sanity.

- Yes. I'd probably use the term faith rather than belief. I knew I wasn't running the show and it had become intuitively obvious to me that Something was.

3. Made a decision to turn our will and our lives over to the care of God as we understood Him.

- Yes, I turned my will over to Whatever was running the show. What's the option when I admitted to myself that I was helpless to end my misery?

4. Made a searching and fearless moral inventory of ourselves.

- Yes, to the best of my ability to do so.

5. Admitted to God, to ourselves, and to another human being the exact nature of our wrongs.

- Yes. I asked an older fellow in AA to be my sponsor, and I went through the list of all my "wrongs" with him. I'd hoped that doing so would produce some internal change, I guess along the lines of relief or freedom, but it left my mind numb for several days. My memory of AA is a blank after that.

Steps 6 thru 8 seem vaguely familiar, but I don't think I went to any more AA meetings after going through step 5 with my sponsor.

Step 1 may be conceptually unimaginable, but all it takes is focusing on some addictive physical or mental process that we don't want to live with, that we've tried unsuccessfully to shake, and we admit to ourselves that we're helpless in the face of that addiction. I was drinking because I was depressed, and I was depressed because I couldn't find that which would relieve my misery. For years I didn't have any words for it, but eventually I saw I was looking for love.

    I couldn't conceive of anything beyond human love, but I could see that no human love would be enough. Intuitively the only hope was in finding that love within, but I'd tried and tried and tried some more, and it wasn't happening. Then a breeze had wafted the conviction into my head that my mentor, Richard Rose, had lost hope in me, so I knew my case was hopeless. That kicked in the depression, and a few years into that I found myself drinking every day during the summer—the warm weather with the sun on my skin made it worse for some reason—two or three drinks a day, just enough to take the edge off. But one day I saw in slow motion that I wasn't in charge of when the daily drinking started or when it stopped… and that it could go downhill very fast. Simultaneously I felt I needed to get around people and recalled that I'd had an interest in working the 12-step program. I called a local AA number and started going to a meeting every day… which lasted for exactly 30 days if I remember right.

    During the depression I often wanted to die, but I also had the conviction that it wasn't right to pray for anything selfish like death. So I was in a corner about praying. When I was having trouble with celibacy during that period was when I would pray… and when I did, HELP would come immediately from within and blast the adversity with unimaginable power.

Do you remember what made this obvious to you (i.e., that Something was running the show rather than the show just running pointlessly on its own)?

I suppose things like the complexity of the universe—it seemed much more likely to me that there was intelligent design, engineering, and maintenance behind it than random accidents—and the impossibility of manifestation: Where did the 1st atom (or quark, lepton, etc.) come from?

My feelings of depression/sadness seem to stem from not having a sense of what my purpose is or what I really want to be doing. I'll get into some project (e.g., musical pursuits, spiritual seeking, recovery, looking for a relationship), but there's always this background feeling of *sigh* "It doesn't really matter..." It occurred to me yesterday that there may be a conviction that my life has no purpose, but I don't feel sure that that's an accurate explanation.

So out of this sadness comes a conflict between half-hearted attempts at things that seem (at least intellectually) worthwhile, and compulsive/addictive attempts at escaping the feeling (i.e., porn or even just visually scanning women). Things get clouded further by the addictive process, since the resulting emotional turbulence makes it harder to tell what I really want or what's just compulsive. There's a mess between "Do I want a relationship because that's what I really want, do I want a relationship because it's an addictive pattern, or do I not really want a relationship, as it's just a procreative urge?"

There seems to be a circular loop here: I'm not willing to admit that I'm helpless, since I'm convinced that I can make it out of the addiction (if there really is an addiction going on... I'm not always sure) if I really try. But since I don't have a sense of what I really want or care about, even recovery carries a sort of "blah, whatever" feeling of indifference in the background, and I never feel like I'm really trying as hard as I could.

The purpose of living is dying. Dying to life is going Home. Dying to untruth is going Home. Home is before and beyond living and dying. I think you know that intuitively, but you lose track of it. Thinking may obscure it for you, particularly emotional thinking.

When/if the mind intuits that "going Home" is its deepest desire, that's a magical time to scan the inner horizon to see if there are any holdouts—competing desires or fears that override the desire to go Home. In either case, the best we can do is to admit honestly to ourselves what we see in moments of relative clarity.

What was the Help like? Did you pray with words, or was it more like an emotional longing?

I don't remember if there were any worded thoughts, but it was an emotional admission and appeal to some inner power or higher self or whatever... I don't think I ever had a name for it. The admission was along the lines of I'm about to be overwhelmed... I've struggled to avoid giving into the compulsion and I see from becoming familiar with the pattern that I'm about to lose the battle... I need Your help, if it's Your will. And instantaneously the game changed: the mental pressure would be removed, and the decision would come out in favor of the desired non-action.

During those moments I didn't kid myself about what I wanted vs. what "it" the adversity (whether it was merely another of "my" desires or the desire of some adverse force) wanted... and I wasn't hypnotized into the belief that I could control it if I wanted to. I knew how the pattern would unfold after it reached a certain point, I knew that point was imminent, and I knew I didn't want it to unfold in that way.

My intuition had awakened when I'd heard Rose say, in the late 1970s, that the answers are within. By then I had achieved the things that I thought should have made me happy, and they weren't enough. For a dozen years I'd been scanning the external horizon, looking for that which would do the job… and not finding anything that held out hope of satisfaction. I didn't know what answer I would find, but I knew then that it could only be found within.

I assume everyone's life-progression has to get to a similar point in order to "see" that the only hope for finding Permanent Satisfaction is if it can be found within, beyond the limitations of this dimension.

~ Art

Show Me How[75]
William Samuel

*Show me how to quench the come and go,
the ebb and flow between serenity and sadness....*

   Listen softly,
I said to the woodman,
   Listen gently with the heart.
   There is no way there but to BE there.
   This way soars above the ground,
   above the landmarks, above the plateaus,
   swiftly, silently, immediately
   on wings of Love.
   This is how I shall take you there, Beloved–
   in an instant
   in the twinkling of an eye
   on the Wings of the Morning.
   Indeed, the Way there is to be there....

---

75 From "The Woodcutter and the King." Thanks to Sandy Jones for permission. See williamsamuel.com for more info about William and his teaching.

You see, Love is the Key to the mystery.
    Love alone sounds the melody
    heard at the immortal Height.
    Love is the wing that lifts thee there
    and there hands thee the scepter.
    Love has beckoned Me, thy Comforter,
    because you and I are One.
    You and I are Love.

Triangulation
To Judy Morrison

When our mind starts to notice the two ends of the paradigm at the same time... that I call triangulation. It is again dis-identification or subtraction with this or that. It is almost like stuff falling off of you... eventually, you are left with basically nothing left to carry. I remember having a long conversation with Art about how triangulation felt to me... almost feels like some other lifetime now... ☺ ... It is not something that you have to work hard for or need to create... but you just realize that the observation point is above duality... you sort of get to the top of the pendulum and can observe the swing instead of being on the swing. An example would be that when you notice happiness, you also realize that an equal amount/intensity of sadness is right there. You only recognize one because you know the opposite of it, too... good/bad; compassion/apathy; beauty/ugliness; love/hate. You stop even pretending to choose this or that... because you see all within... the two sides of the same coin.

If you didn't know summer, would you recognize winter? Can there be a day without the night? As we keep taking a step back, the view keeps getting bigger... and if it is in your view, it can't be you. Not this, not this.[76]

~ Anima, December 20, 2011.
(We had initially collected most of the material for this book in that year, but then we let it (and us) age and have now distilled it for consumption.)

---
[76] Neti neti, a keynote of Vedic inquiry. With its aid the Jnani negates identification with all things of this world.

An Interesting Dream

I had to share this dream that I had this morning between 6:30 am and 7:30 am.

I dreamt that Art, Sharad, Todd, me, (Cecy was around but not participating), and a few more people (including one of my sisters) are having a self-inquiry meeting at the Rose farm, but the room is really small... with the kind of lights, yellowish, that we use in India. The mood of the place is not at all tense but very sort of friendly and affectionate.

There is a break... Cecy offers to make food. I am teasing her by telling her I want to eat kadhi-chawal[77]... she tells me to go to hell. Cecy, you were wearing one of those long Victorian dresses with frills... but not bosom showing :)... high collars... bright color.

And then all of us are taking a nap... there are no lights in the room... my sister is lying next to me... and suddenly my mind I feel has sort of flipped. Suddenly I feel I have no boundaries... my mind is coming and going out of this state... I am scared to open my eyes because I know it will see things that it is not used to seeing... and when I do open my eyes, I see my sister's dream. She is fighting a demon... sort of kicking him. I am keeping my eyes shut because I know when I open my eyes... I will be gone. It is not a pleasant experience nor an unpleasant experience. I am seeing things in a very different dimension... it is as if I have become open to a different dimension .... and a funny sound is coming out of my mouth, but nobody is waking up. And then Cecy wakes up, and she and I hold hands and go out. There is a river... green grass... and I see a big gray rabbit. I know that

---

[77] Rice and curry made with gram flour.

Cecy knows that my mind is not in its boundaries right now .... and I know she is not seeing what I am seeing. Everything looks very bright and silent. And at that moment I know my small mind is not ready to die and wants a familiar universe. And yet I feel it is free. It is a very impersonal experience. I can see my small mind and feel its fears and still there is the feeling of no boundaries feeling.

Interesting!!!! I swear I didn't cook this up... the dream was very real... but my body woke up. :(

~ Anima, June 28, 2000

A Letter to My Younger Self

Hello anima,

I understand that you are at that point in life where any hope of finding happiness ever again seems unlikely. Life has become a burden. Even the slightest ray of 'hope' right now feels painful. You just want to disappear forever. Not having to wake up tomorrow seems like a respite-full idea.

Life happens. You have seen how temporary and impermanent this life-charade is. No matter how much you want any happy experience to continue, it doesn't. Maybe it is a good thing. Because it means the not so happy moment will also get over at some point. Though painful times always feel much longer, the fact remains that all beginnings have an end.

This acute dissatisfaction within, which you had thought would go away with this new relationship, job, place, or cool toy, seems to be a state that you can't get rid of. No matter what you do. It gets harder to distract yourself from this inner void. I know often you think of ending this all for good by simply killing yourself. This will probably be a way of showing Life that you are not a victim. You will not have to tolerate this pain anymore. A few extra pills and then the peaceful sleep forever.

But what if this nightmare does not end. What if, just like everything else, this peaceful, permanent sleep that you so much want right now, is also temporary. You know from experience that there is nothing permanent about this reality. As you understand yourself better, you realize that all this pain and suffering you had thought was coming from outside is really within. Outside is only mirroring inside.

Buddha said that suffering is the essential fire that burns the impurities of the gold for it to become pure. I know right now you can't appreciate the fact that if you weren't in this prison of life, you would have no interest in wanting Freedom. Or if all this means anything at all. I know you smirk when you read advice from Ramana to put your baggage down when traveling on a train. Your precious baggage of unmet expectations, punctured projections, unfulfilled desires, unsaid words, hurtful sentences, humiliations, broken pride. Do you realize you are addicted to your story of suffering? This story is who you are. This is your identity. Expecting you to be able to see that anything could be outside of this prison would not be fair. But you do have the desire to become Free. If you are expecting that the path that you are seriously contemplating to take will lead you to freedom, then, my friend, you may be wrong. Taking away your life may not be the answer.

I do not know what will happen to you if you decide to sleep tonight, but my suspicion is that the dream, if the dreamer doesn't Wake up, will continue. And what do you expect the next turn in the dream will be? What I am saying to you, idiot-me, is listen to that tiny inner voice. This might be your opportunity to become Freedom, to become Absolute, to become Love. There is a reason why life is unfolding for you the way it is. What do you feel it is trying to teach you? What is the direction it is making you go?

Now the good news: Hitting rock bottom, if survived, you become serious about really finding the Absolute Answer to ALL your problems. You know that nothing short of a complete Answer can cure you of this pain. The little voice inside is saying that this season will pass also. Thank god impermanence is the nature of this existence. When you have clarity about what your purpose in life is, you will realize that the universe aligns itself to assist you towards the final end of your journey.

If you are reading this, then I assume you know what I am talking about. Characters might be different, but the screenplay is more or less the same. I have found that the mind is an amazing gift that you have been given. Learn to use it wisely or else it can cause irreparable damage. Don't become a victim of sheer physiology. Your mind will find the Answer to the Question you ask. What question are you asking?

When all feels dark, just remember Me…

I want to be able to write this letter to you, so don't deprive me of this opportunity. And please be kind. Everyone you meet is fighting a hard battle, says Plato.

~ Anima

※

A friend and fellow-seeker, who had been active in TAT and in the Pittsburgh self-inquiry group in the middle years of the previous decade along with several of us still active in TAT, committed suicide in April 2020. That event prompted Anima to write the above letter for the *TAT Forum*, to any seekers who find themselves contemplating an intentional ending of their life.

~ Art

A Change of Heart

There's a whisper in the wind...
Can you hear it calling?
Can you make out what it's saying?
There's a scent on the wind...
Wafting as from another time and place,
Stirring faint memory of something long ago.
There's a feeling in the air...
Of a lost Eden, of our original home
Before time drew us
Into its attractive and maddening seeming.
We long to go back,
To return to perfection,
But who knows the way?
It requires a change of heart.
We've been living a great lie.
We gradually discard its props,
The make-believe personality
With its prides and fears that rise
Along with separation anxiety.
The distinction between self and others
Softens as the perceived differences wane.
The connection to our source strengthens
As the self diminishes.
O Love, we cry, where are you hiding?
And in the mist of miracle
We find ourselves back home,
Awake from the dream of separation.

~ Art

Love Letter to God/Highest Self

Dear Highest "Me,"

How long will I be away? When will I know or become the Unseparated One? (That is You.) It's lonely down here and also tiring. My longing is distraction to hide the pain of existence away from my consciousness because it is too overwhelming. I would lose myself if that pain were to engulf me—and that pain is Love but appears to me as Death + Impermanence.

I feel you at times whispering softly in my ear; the call to awaken has not been ignored—but my own shouts are unanswered. Frustration, exhaustion, silence, silence… and I am still here wishing for my own absolvation* (being solved like a formula mixing into the whole). What is your wish for me? Am I even? Or just odd? Yeah, you have a better sense of humor than me, but it appears as tragedy and pain, pain that is too much, and I say "no more."

When, I ask again, will it, or I that am not, end? When?

❦

*Absolvation is an uncommon variation of absolution, carrying the meaning of being dissolved at the same time as the self coming apart but also merging into that which is. Absolution is not the right word here. The root of solve (meaning to loosen or unfasten) with the prefix ab- meaning "away from" meaning loosening away from myself into Myself.

P.S. Two weeks and two days later after the exercise and writing of this letter, the answer came in a dream: "I love you... And there is no time."

~ Ricky Cobb III, as part of a group retreat exercise

True Love

I was talking with some friends the other day about *rapport* and remembered my first experience of it. I had taken my son for a vacation in the Bahamas to celebrate his nineteenth birthday, and the small hotel we were staying at was populated mostly by college students on spring break. Our first evening there we joined a group that had congregated around the courtyard pool and found immediate acceptance from them.

There were a dozen or so of us, about evenly split between males and females. We fell into a pattern of doing things together in smaller groups during the day then meeting at the pool around dusk. After indulging in relaxed merriment and comparing notes about our adventures while apart, we'd all head out to some public place where there was music or to a private party that someone knew about.

One of the group was a young woman from Boston who I noticed would always be sitting quietly next to me but with whom I'd had no direct interaction. On what may have been our second evening together, the whole group moved from our hotel to a club in one of the large, colonial-era hotels, which had a dance floor and live music. The quiet girl, Lorna, again sat silently next to me when our group spread itself among available tables. So I asked her if she'd like to dance. She said yes, or possibly just nodded her head, and we moved onto the small dance floor. It was a slow dance, and as soon as we embraced, there were no longer two minds; there was one mind encompassing two bodies, each of which was experiencing the same thoughts and feelings, knowing that the other body was experiencing the same thoughts and feelings: like an infinite regression between two mirrors. As soon as we had embraced, it was as if a wave went out from us and radiated across the room. It was felt by one of the musicians in the combo behind me who said, *sotto voce*, "True love."

That diminishment of separation is an indicator of what we're intuitively looking for, which is to escape our painful identification as a separate creature that was born, is under constant threat of annihilation, and is inevitably going to die. But it didn't last. When the dance was over and we returned to the table, so was the rapport.

The next evening when we gathered at the pool and saw each other again, it was almost as if Lorna and I didn't like each other. George, a hotel employee with whom we'd become friendly, volunteered to take our group to a local club, and we all jumped on the offer. It turned out to be in the boondocks and was populated strictly by local folks, who looked unhappy to see us there. But they became friendly after the initial shock wore off, and we had a good time. After that we returned to town (Nassau) and found a crowded, disco-type club. Lorna and I were still avoiding each other, but I eventually spotted her in the crowd when a slow dance started and asked her to dance. As soon as we embraced, we were again one mind. It was even more intense this time. We ignored whatever music was playing, barely moving our feet as we held each other tight for what may have been an hour or more, until the club closed. Then we walked back to the hotel arm in arm, silently.

The next morning, the entire group assembled outside the hotel to say goodbye to Lorna and her friends when the taxi came to take them to the airport. She and I didn't exchange information to keep in touch. Altogether we probably hadn't said more than ten or twenty words to each other.

Is it possible to find the complete and full satisfaction that experiences like the above point to? Ironically, what we're looking for—love, security, permanence, meaning, or however it becomes represented in the mind—is what we find when we recognize our true identity. Seeking conscious awareness of our essential being, and helping others do the same, is the ultimate purpose and meaning for our lives. Our real identity is that which we're seeking: True, never-ending Love.

~ Art

Full Moon

The moon was full last night,
did you notice it...
I think it is that crazy moon playing tricks
with Radha's[78] heart...

Since it is just going out of bounds...
with ecstatic happiness...
She knows not how to deal with it...
or what to do with herself...
her feet are not touching the floor...
should she just die this very moment...
'cause she doesn't want it to pass

She finally feels she belongs, I think...
she knew surrender today...
and she lived eternity
in a moment...
and now there is nothing else left...
for her to dance to....

You know... that dusht[79] trickster Shyam,[80]
who has stolen her heart from her...
got tricked into making her his....
maybe he is just teasing her...
like he always does...

---
78 A popular and revered goddess in Hinduism, worshipped as the goddess of love, tenderness, compassion and devotion.
79 Wicked.
80 Krishna, known as Shyam to those who find beauty, wisdom, and love in his dark complexion.

that dukhdayi[81] Shyam...
what should I do with him...
is it possible
to love him just a little less...

~ Anima

---
81   Irksome.

The Bhakti Doorway

Loving (people, animals, god) is one side of the equation. In a way it's the easier side. Receiving love from people and feeling god's love is often harder. We react with fear of losing ourselves, fear of being overwhelmed, obligations, and so on. Both sides of the equation contain the belief in self and other. And then there's *being* love... our origin and destination.

~ Art

Unity

In Harding's experiments it is my sense that they are designed to open your eyes to a first-person (not true first person, but creating a perceived discrepancy in what you think you are and your closer truth of first-person experience, thereby opening you to the possibility that you've always been "mistaken" so to speak.) How is a first-person experience of unity possible? I can't really say unity is possible as it hasn't been my experience. Are there exercises to allow it to become my experience?

I think the closest we get to unity as a personal experience is not-twoness.

When I experienced not-twoness when slow-dancing with Lorna in the Bahamas at age 38,[82] it was as if we were one mind experiencing the same thoughts and feelings and knowing that Lorna knew that I knew that she knew... like an infinite series of reflections in two facing mirrors. I suspect that's similar to what Bernadette Roberts experienced as oneness with God as a 25-year-old Discalced Carmelite nun and what Jill Bolte Taylor, the Harvard neurological researcher, experienced at age 37 when a hemorrhagic stroke flooded the left hemisphere of her brain, including the visual cortex, and she could no longer detect edges separating herself from the view.

The only true unity is Being—our essential identity.

~ Art

---

82 See "True Love" above.

9

And in the End

I Am Always Right Behind You
Verses from May 10, 2004

I am always right behind you
But turn around and you won't see me
I am never not with you.
Why aren't you always with me?

I am at the center
while you stay at the periphery
I am there, too,
but you won't find me there.
When you turn round
the center stays behind you
Stand still while turning your gaze around
and look at what you're looking out of.

❦

Are you looking for love?
Love on the periphery is partial and fleeting
When you are with me
We are not two—and I am Love Absolute.

Are you afraid of dying?
I created you to think you are living
Return to Me here, at the center
and find your undying Self.

Are you pursuing understanding?
It's a path to Truth

And in the End

But conceptual understanding is of the periphery
To return to the center is a subtractive process,
leaving behind the pride of knowing.

※

Looking for love?
Keep looking and it will find you
It may not be what you expect
but it will be satisfying beyond your imagining.

※

Forget what you're looking for?
That may be a good sign.
Keep looking.

~ Art

Always Right Behind You

To Anima on May 17, 2004

Dear Friend,

Feeling great. Will attach some details on the retreat.
Poem for you that came into my head the other day:

The Rajput warrior princess
is now a mama-queen
With infant prince and princess
for her to feed and wean.
Then as they get older
she'll resume her search
for that which is between.

~ Art (which is funny, since he was never really alive....:)

Questions Answered

From Anima
June 03, 2004
Art,

Are you out of your bed yet. About an hour back i think i got to experience something. i have been awake since 3 am. Around 5.20 am... how should i explain... there was this alive darkness where this physical organism was pretty scared to go. it is just here that aliveness... how do i explain what I experienced. mind has nothing to do with it. it is right here and this ghost just doesn't want to look at it. how do i tell you. i was lying in my bed. just having mental chatter about this and that and then at some point my mind had this thought about trying to get a feel of God... words that popped in my head: "I wonder what God feels like," and suddenly it was there... right in my ears and behind this forehead... all over... this physical organism was not comfortable at all... kept trying to turn away from it... and yet couldn't... it is not me or you art... it is All....

everybody is still sleeping... have been wanting to call you... heart feels heavy...

thanks...
ghost/shadow...

From Art
June 03, 2004
Anima,

"... my mind had this thought about trying to get a feel of God....and suddenly it was there" – That's all it may take. It's what we are, so it can be seen by anyone who wants to stop looking away from it. Nothing prevents it. But we can't will it.

You know me well enough to know that you can call any time, day or night, and I'd be happy to hear from you. Even at 3:30 AM... :)

You're young enough that seeing it may be traumatic. To me, seeing it, and then eventually accepting it, was 100% relief.

From Anima
June 29, 2004
Hello my dearest friend,

My heart has been so joyous these days in spite of little irritations caused by all these junior and senior Borles... :). everyone is taking a nap right now. It is so quiet for a change.

After that morning my head went into a state of shock almost, for a few days, with questions like how could it happen to me... etc. Found myself wanting to go into that state again. re-lived the experience through my memory bank every now and then. After that, ego got perked up with wow... 'i' must have done something right kind of feeling.... :) It is funny to watch all these reactions. There is no better entertainment

And in the End

then your own little head... i have all the drama equivalent to any soap opera... :).

These days i am back into the two little babies... busy changing diapers and playing mommy... :)

Told my mother and Sharad about it. My mom got all worried that i am on the verge of leaving my kids... :) Sharad, as usual, tried to see pros and cons.

Art, there is only one thing that i am sure of... if it wasn't for you... i would still be wandering in my mind alleys. It was your email that brought to my attention to "try to get the feel instead of paying attention to the words." That night i found myself wondering what Art had meant by that and how to get beyond words when that experience happened. You really don't need any of the senses to experience that state. Mind actually is as mechanical as any other organ of our body and the physical body in some way resists. I don't know what word to use... the experience for me lasted for about 10 minutes, I am not sure... time felt still. Little anima must have accumulated some good karma while she was around to have met you... you are the best teacher i could ever have asked for.

The No-Head Circle

*I*n 1947, a month after his self-realization, Richard Rose wrote to a friend:

> *I am glad that you are in accord with the idea of forming a circle. Let us at least call it a circle... something without a head or tail... a ring of equality.*

That was Rose's ideal for a group of people working together on the grand project of knowing the self, which became the basis for the TAT Foundation that he formed in 1973.

Douglas Harding embodied the "no-head circle" concept into an experiment.[83] Try this sometime with a few friends:

- Stand in a circle with some friends—between say 3 and 10 of you. Put your arms round each other so that you are close, and look down.
- There you see a circle of bodies. Obviously they are distinct from one another, each taking their own space. They do not merge into some kind of 'oneness'. Each body there has a name, a background and history, an age, a nationality and so on. Down there we are separate from one another.
- Notice your own body—it disappears above the chest into No-thingness.

---

83 See https://www.headless.org/experiments/no-head-circle.html Thanks to Richard Lang.

- Notice that from this point of view the other bodies also disappear above their chests—into the same No-thingness that your body disappears into.
- Here at the top there are not many No-things—just one. Here in this edgeless space are no dividing lines, no name tags, no bit of the No-thing that is mine or yours. Here we are indivisibly one.
- The nameless awareness here at the top includes all those different bodies. They all disappear into, or emerge out of, this One who has no name.
- Looking down, each of us has our own unique point of view, our own thoughts and feelings. I don't know what you are thinking, or what your past is. I might not even know your name. But I can see who you really are—here at the top of the circle.

- Here at the top all our differences dissolve, all separation is overcome—without destroying those differences down there. The space at the top has room for every point of view.
- The No-Head Circle is like a circular temple. The bodies form the walls, like columns. But this temple is ruined—the roof has been blown clear off. The temple lies wide-open to the sky—a sky that is totally clear. A sky that is boundless. You are that infinite sky—the sky of Being.
- Who is it that now looks down?
- Looking at the Looker I come home to who I really am, the One who has no boundaries, and I find that this One includes everyone. Down there in the circle I am one amongst many—others stand either side of me, apart from me, with me, perhaps even against me. But here, above the line of chests, there are no others. All divisions are healed, all separation overcome.
- Here, looking down, including us all, is the One within all beings. You are that One.

Dear reader: Please note that reading about this experiment doesn't do the trick. Try it, and see if it causes a shift in your paradigm. The same caveat applies to all spiritual reading. To be helpful it must inspire action, which ultimately means looking for yourself.

In friendship,
Art

Hearing

O incomprehensible not-twoness,
Whose music is the silent hum
upon which the ears and the sound waves of the universe ride,
Where within thee is hearing, where the phantom hearer?

~ Art

Roadmap of My Inner Path

Life Soup

- Experiences, reactions, actions, driven by desires, fears, pride and sense of entitlement.
- Realization that I am an unfulfilled, incomplete, restless being.
- Life is lived with a hope that tomorrow will be better than today.
- The natural urge to be Happy and Peaceful... Completely and Permanently.

Introspection

- Why am I so miserable?
- Pursuits and attainments do not lead to Happiness.
- The situational change will not be satisfactory.
- Transiency of life cannot be ignored

Inner Landscape

- Messy emotions.
- Mechanical/reactive living.
- Enslaved by my desires and fears.

Self-Observation

- Observing my life experiences.
- Trying to understand the why of my reactions and actions.
- Discerning the problem:
  - The reason for my suffering does not lie outside.
  - 'One-pointed Vector'. – Richard Rose
  - Only when we have discerned the problem do we become an open-eyed seeker. – Vedanta
- Discerning the Solution
  - The permanent solution to my suffering has to be found within.
  - The desire for FREEDOM from all wants and limitations.
  - Wanting Truth at all costs.

self-Inquiry

- The effort to understand what this suffering is and how to end it.
- Who is this that suffers?
- Body-mind, personality, decision-making processes, and emotional drama comes into the view.
- The effort to know is directly proportional to the intensity of life experience.
- Leads to dis-passion, detachment, and dis-identification with your story and yourself.

Self-Inquiry

- Want to know God/Truth for no other reason than to know.
- self/I shrinks; doer disappeared.
- No addition or subtraction is needed.
- No other place to go.
- No one else can do it for you.
- There is no magical technique or practice that will do it for you.
- The only problem is 'you'.
- The mind feels finally serious.

Self-Awareness

- Glimpses/experiences that are not created by your five senses or mind.
- Awareness of I am a Witness and Witnessing.
- The realization that all experiences are in Awareness, including you.
- Sense of eternal being-ness that is changeless.
- Yet, why is Awareness still individualized?
- Lingering doubt.

Self-Realization

- Attention shifts from self to Self.
- Transcendence from self.

- There is direct knowledge, a different kind of knowing.
- You are No-thing and All things.

Self-remembrance

- I Am.

~ Anima

Freedom

When we stay conscious and watch thoughts and feelings, does it mean they don't affect us at all? What is the goal I need to aspire to by staying conscious? Is it to have no thoughts because I'm fully attentive to just being? For me it requires a lot of concentration to do that, and I can only hold it so long until thoughts rush in and I'm lost again. Are thoughts my enemy?

Consciously watching thoughts/feelings diminishes their hypnotic effect. We get temporary distance from them—like taking a step back from being too close to a painting on the wall—before being caught up in them again. The goal of observing is to realize that what we're seeing is not what sees—i.e., not the self, which we're intuitively looking for as the solution to our problems. We don't know whether we'll experience no-thought, or whether no thought is necessary. Thinking is addictive... we're afraid of no thought/no feeling.

I think one thing that makes me recoil from Richard Rose's writings is because he presents this business of self-inquiry as a fierce fight, like the last battle of Hector versus Achilles in the movie Troy. The older I get, the less of a warrior I become, although I can still be obsessive about things. The obsession I cannot control; but lately I have been wondering what acquisition (this word I used to qualify the term "reward") is so worth my anxieties and sufferings. On one hand, I question whether kindness to others is important for Rose. On the other, I am aware of the most likely possibility that I am reading too much into what he is saying based on my image of Rose as being harsh (which I don't know where I got it from).

And in the End

As Richard Rose would have been the first to admit, there are two broad paths to Full Satisfaction: self-inquiry and surrender—fighter and lover. He thought the best path for most guys was the path of doubt and fighting, and that's what most of his writing is focused on. That was his path. The final step for everyone is surrender. The bhakti path is more aligned with that approach. My feeling is that while the self-inquirer is trying to find her self, the bhakta is trying to lose her self. Both paths are fraught with difficulties and succeed through failure. The key ingredient, I believe, is persistence in whatever path we're drawn to.

Rose, by the way, was a very kindhearted person who could also be ferocious. He had such a soft character that he determined, as a teenager, never to let anyone intimidate him again. He used to have to cross the street in order to avoid losing energy (i.e., he was overly sympathetic) as a young person when he'd see certain people coming down the sidewalk toward him.

"For a year and a half, he rose at four o'clock every morning to work on his novel before a full day of seeing patients."[From a biographical sketch about the author of The Kite Runner.*] But the author could conceive of a clear positive reward. It could be the case that the writing itself is the reward. I used to feel this when I got excited about a project, and hence could not wait for the time I could work on it. But if there is no reward to be gained, or the goal is conceived in terms of a loss (of suffering), then it's hard to imagine being active or in the offense. I don't think self-inquiry is a joyful path. How can I be excited about it?*

Your mind-self, which wants to maintain the status quo of pretense and illusion, has latched onto the concept that the goal of self-inquiry involves loss or suffering. That mind-self will pursue its objective of unconditional love in what it regards as a safe way until it comes to the realization that it's not going to work. My advice is to accelerate that pursuit by facing fears.

There are two ways to buy a car, for example: saving for it until you can pay entirely, or financing it and paying over several years. If we were practical, we'd put a cap of maybe six months of income on what we'd spend... and save that amount before purchase. We may feel that's a joyless path, and one of self-deprivation compared with financing the most expensive vehicle we can and enjoying it now. (Being in the now. :-) So we end up spending maybe twice as much for the vehicle and are under the gun to make the payments each month, worrying about how to juggle all the competing payments due, worrying about what will happen if we lose our job, and so on.

Self-inquiry leads to oneness with what we are at the core of our being. At the core of our being is complete freedom. The path to freedom is one of diminishing enslavement to addictions, both physical and mental. At the core of our being we don't find the love we were looking for as separate, lonely, vulnerable beings... we find that we are love.

~ Art

Credo
"I Believe"

BEFORE:
I believe that...

- I am a person
- I am conscious of a world outside myself
- I was born into this preexisting world
- The world continues when I'm sleeping
- My body is still here when I'm sleeping
- I'm experiencing another dimension when I'm dreaming
- I am an unconscious body when in dreamless sleep
- My core attribute is consciousness or awareness of things
- I hope that awareness continues after my body dies

AFTER:
I know that...

- I am
- Have always been
- Timeless
- The source of time
- Changeless

Always Right Behind You

- The source of change
- Dimensionless
- The source of space
- Nothing
- The source of the first thing and of all things

~ Art

Are You Free?

Are you free?

I Am.
I have found that I am not what can become Free or can be in Bondage.

Do you want to know if I am free of my headaches/relationship problems/daily irritations, etc.? Then, no... I still yell at my kids, cry when my grandmother dies, have emotions, have a horrible personality, etc.

Do you want to know if I have found what I assume you are looking for... Truth? I found that I already was what I was seeking.

I used to think I was looking for God/Truth, but basically I just wanted freedom from my suffering... which I found much sooner than I found God, but then I realized that wasn't going to cut it for me.

So my friend, if freedom from suffering is your goal, then you'll find it very-very easily as you walk this path.

~ Anima

Nothing and Everything

The seed of wisdom did I sow
And with mine own hand wrought to make it grow;
And this was all the harvest that I reaped –
I came like water, and like wind I go.
~ Omar Khayyam, *The Rubáiyát*

The individual comes out of nothing and returns to nothing....
Nothing remains....
Nothing remains, *unchanged*....
Nothing is *that which really is*....
Self-aware

~ Art

Man Reads a Book

Man reads a book or watches a film and finds feelings that his heart aspires to: *"I am helpless myself, God alone is all powerful, and except by throwing myself completely on Him, there is no other means of safety for me,"* for example. Man is literally moved by those feelings, the shift taking place inside.

1. Man finds those feelings inside himself, finds that all feelings he has ever experienced are inside himself.
2. Man finds that he is That which experiences... not that which is experienced.
3. Man forgets. Then he remembers. Remembering then forgetting is painful.
4. His longing becomes steadier, burning away resistance to the final kneeling to the truth.

"His is the burden. You have no longer any cares. All your cares are His. Such is surrender. That is bhakti."[84]

~ Art

---

84 The two quotes are of Ramana Maharshi, in *Gems from Bhagavan.*

Dear Friend

Dear friend,
On a path of returning Home,
who is going to show you
around your own house?
How long will you keep turning your head away
from looking at your own Self?

Are you afraid that
this sense of "I",
my body, mind, thoughts, emotions,
and this experience of life,
which you take yourself to be,
will disappear?
The dream will end?
The story, your story, is a lie?

When you become a moth —
drawn to the flame,
willingly flying into your end,
without changing the course,
merging into the burning flame,
becoming one with the Source —
shell burns.
You don't.

You just have to stop and look
only for a moment,
and It will do the rest,
It will pull you in.

And in the End

You don't need to do anything.
One step you take towards It,
four steps It jumps towards you.

I can see Me
sparkling in your eyes.
Can you see You in mine?
You, the Pure Being,
the Center of the universe,
beyond all opposition and duality,
needs no inclusion or subtraction.

You are the Source,
the Flame in all.
Just stop and look, if you can.
At least give it a try,
my dear, dear friend,
while I hold your hand
and you hold mine.

~ Anima

The Purpose of Life

One time in a talk at one of the universities in Raleigh, while he was packing up at the end of the Q&A session, a woman in the audience asked Richard Rose what he thought about love. Ordinarily he would respond to questions about love with something flippant or confrontational, but he picked up a genuine, non-sales intent about her question and answered: Well, the purpose of life is love... but we haven't got time to go into it here.

Love was not a topic that Rose talked about much. He did express the view that there are two general paths to Truth, that of the fighter and that of the lover. I believe he thought most men should become fighters.

What did he mean by "the purpose of life is love"? I had a vague feeling of what he was referring to then, but now my guess would be that he was pointing to the feeling that the ultimate purpose of individual life-experience is the journey back to Self... like the raindrop's journey back to the ocean.

~ Art

The Dreamer

Last night
just as soon as my head hit the pillow
I was asleep.
And in my sleep, I had a dream
of mountains and valleys,
rivers and streams.
I dreamt of friends
and people from the past and present.
Look, it's me.
I am right there as well,
Traveling on the bus through mountains
with a friend,
The heart filled with glee.

Interestingly,
the dream character, me,
has no idea how unreal it is
A figment of someone's dream.
Immersed in the story,
clueless of its reality,
is feeling a full range of emotions,
deciphering the riddles of life
being fully alive.

The next morning as I wake up
I remember the dream
and the dream character, me.

The funny thing about these me-dreams
Is that the dream character

Always Right Behind You

always is seeking something,
Or trying to get to someplace.
Without ever finding what it seeks.
There is just a constant anxious movement,
running from one post to the other.

Dreamer, me, experiences
what the dream character goes through.
Hoping that in one of these dreams
the dream character, me
will wake up to its unreality.
Not realizing that it is
the dreamer who must wake up
to end the dream.

I can see that my daydream
Is not very different from the night dream.
I am again projecting the world
and me in it
then reacting to my own projections.

Am I the dream character again
in my own dream.

~ Anima

Burning Intensity

I often prayed—and pray—for a burning intensity that will consume completely.

What consumes us is love. Personal love consumes us relatively; God's love (Truth) consumes our limitations.

~ Art

I Who Speak
Franklin Merrell-Wolff

SOMETIMES AS I WRITE, the I becomes We and yet remains I.

There is a Consciousness which, while It remains One, is a symphony of harmoniously blended parts.

I write, and *I* watch myself writing.

I know, and yet I wonder at the knowing.

I am the student and, at the same time, *I* am the Teacher.

As Teacher, *I* stand in Majesty looking upon the world below.

As student, I look up, humbly and amazed.

I speak and, presently, there blends with my voice the melodious Voices of Others.

One Meaning in many tones is unfolded.

So the tones of the seven-stringed Lyre are all sounded; one here, another there, in groups and, finally, all together.

And before this Melody I sit entranced, filled to the brim and more.

I who Speak none ever will know until, on that final Day he finds Himself, when *I* will appear in all My Glory.[85]

---

85 From *Pathways Through to Space*. Thanks to Doroethy Leonard.

The "NO" Poem

There are no doubts left,
No unanswered questions,
No fears,
No desires,
No unfulfilled dreams,
No unsung songs,
No you, nor me.

~ Anima

10
Epilogues

Seekers' Stories from Friends Who Have Passed

*F*ive of the friends we've worked with have since passed on. They had written biographical sketches of their searches as part of our self-inquiry email group exchanges in the 2005 to 2011 period, and we'd like to share them with you as memorials to these friends whom we miss.

S. B.
September 2005
I've been on a spiritual path, on and off, since 1971. Met Richard Rose in the fall of '72 and started working with the group in '73. Took several hiatuses over the years, sometimes lasting several years, but couldn't shake this stuff and was lucky enough to not get trapped into a wife and kids. Lived with Art in Miami back in the mid 80's, then went back to school and Art moved to the farm. Kind of lost touch with the group after that. Then about 3 years ago Art sent me a notice about a TAT meeting and I decided to go. I was inspired and worked with the group for a while, but left one more time. Came back again I guess a year or so ago and have been working with the group ever since. Dates may be a little off, but I think you get the point. Nothing else of importance to tell you about my life.

September 2006 update
Spiritual action over the last 9 months: Spiritually speaking, the last nine months have culminated into deciding to take a new approach toward spiritual work. Instead of working toward attaining self-realization, I will work toward being as

honest to myself as I possibly can without regard to attaining anything. Outwardly not much will change. For now I intend on practicing meditation, do group work and practice self-awareness but without the pretense of being a spiritual seeker. So far the hardest part is letting go of this possible reward (enlightenment). It's still in my mind but I reason that I don't really know what enlightenment or self-realization means so why use that as a goal?

Along with this new attitude means a change in lifestyle. I'm not sure yet what that involves, but I'm pretty sure that it will involve becoming a more social human being, more outgoing and less introverted.

Meditation seems like an extremely important practice, more than any other practice that I mentioned earlier. So my commitment is to meditate 1 hour/day.

꽃

S. B. died in May 2014 after several years of decline from familial spastic paraplegia. He was a good friend of mine for many, many years. I saw him for the last time in 2013. He was one of the kindest and gentlest people I've ever known. ~ Art

I was in an accountability group with S. B. Also met him a few times during TAT retreats. Found him to be quiet and introspective. ~ Anima

J. M.
December 2011
I spent many years, starting in my 20's, reading extensively, trying to understand what this enlightenment thing was about. My questions, the ones mind can answer, weren't really answered til I found TAT in about 2004, which was

definitely the most significant event. That was also my first encounter with real, ordinary people who had found the final answer, although I had traveled to meet several teachers and attend retreats or satsangs. For the most part my method has been reading and contemplating what I've read, researching ideas, and searching inside for insight and understanding of these. I've also done this AR [we called the weekly reports we sent each other "accountability reports"; in addition to asking questions one week then responding to them the following week, participants also gave updates on activities they wanted the group to help them be accountable for] several years, participated in a couple of other online spiritual groups, and emailed with different TAT people. I've not done much formal meditation, though I now feel that many times what I was doing was a type of meditation.

At this point, most of the time I am aware of myself as a sort of automatically operating meatball with thoughts, with a mysterious presence there behind it all, doing I know not what. When I occasionally fall back into belief that I am choosing or creating, it doesn't take long to remember (and usually be amused at) that busy little insignificant meatball. Creeping into this more and more is a sense that pride in being the doer (ha) is imprisoning me, and that surrender is our natural state, being fended off by pride. When the urge to "do some work" arises, many times a day, I look—for the me that it feels like I am, or at the mysterious presence, mostly. This usually ends with my feeling powerless and frustrated: "what am I doing? 'I' can't do it." I try to sustain this looking for 30-minute periods, particularly upon arising, but this is an uphill battle. In recent years, what I call glimpses have revealed what I consider the actual truth of several things, such as, observing is constant and forever, and all things are of equal value or weight. It seems to me we get these peeks into reality, through no effort of our own, as our only actual indication that what we seek is the only reality.

I am old and my health is not the best. I don't have a lot of hope that the final answer will come. But I have no other purpose and could not possibly stop trying.

※

J. M. died in April 2017. J. M. and I were friends. We did women's retreats together, met at TAT retreats, also worked together in the accountability group. I always felt she was serious and yet turned away when she got close. I had a feeling that it was her deep attachment to her son that made her stay on the fence. ~ Anima

After J. M. could no longer travel to West Virginia for TAT meetings and retreats, we kept in touch. In the winters of 2012 and 2013 I visited her and S. B. when I made trips through Georgia to Florida from West Virginia, and after I moved to Florida in 2013, we'd see each other at least once or twice a year, which was always a joy for me, and by email between visits. ~ Art

J. C.
September 2005
I first started down this path of self-inquiry about 4 or was it 5 years ago when I started attending meetings held by Art in Pittsburgh while I was in college. Posters he put up made me vaguely curious. What weighed most heavily on my mind at the time was what am I going to do with my life, and that is still something I am insecure about. Since then I have done a lot of group work (accountability and self-inquiry reports, group meetings, individual retreats) but not so much

Epilogues

individual work comparatively. I feel like if I am really going to talk about me and what has defined me, much of the time in my life in general it's moods and states of mind. They have tended to dominate me. When a certain mood comes on, a feeling state, it produces a corresponding thought state, which is where much of my attention and energy goes. I tend by a large degree to be caught up in the internal movie as opposed to the external one—I'm often pretty oblivious of the outside world. A mood of sadness and emptiness sometimes just overtakes me, and it tends to be something I don't want to face. In general I think I tend to run from such emotions. Where I currently find myself is wanting to get out of the pattern I have been in for so long of being subject to my moods and often hypnotized by them. There is also a basic insecurity that I have that I am more aware of. At this point I feel like I don't like writing an intro—maybe because I've said stuff like this before and I am not really sure about whether I am seeing myself clearly or not. One of the feelings I have right now is that I just don't know what is going on.

Things that are more concrete and easier to talk about… I've been out of college for a couple years now and have worked a variety of jobs: house construction, team-building/environmental education with kids, and a research assistant at the Federal Reserve Board of Governors. The first two I took mainly to face fears and also to live out what I thought the ideal person would do. The last job is in line with one of my majors (economics) and more typical for someone with my general abilities. Since college I've lived in Louisville KY and Washington DC and in both places started self-inquiry discussion groups for mixed reasons. Those have been hard generally, sometimes enjoyable and sometimes helpful to me and others (from what they've said). These are one of the places I've seen that I am much more comfortable with concepts and ideas than with emotions. Soon I will be moving back to Pittsburgh and living in the ashram there, and for work I most likely will be doing part-time teaching and tutoring, which I generally look forward to.

Other things that are probably worth mentioning are that I have been celibate almost my entire life and have generally been afraid of girls/women most of my life. I have never really been in a relationship... I dated a girl for a month in college and it was a very tension-filled time. Again reflecting a basic insecurity, which much in my life has seemed to reflect lately.

I guess I am caught in a mood right now because I feel like I may have just said nothing about myself or that much of what I said may not be true. I can imagine being in a different state of mind and possibly writing different things. I don't feel like I have an objective or even relatively objective view. Writing this intro has by far been the most confrontational part of this report and it has brought up a good amount of anger (at having to write it).

January 2007 return
Hi everyone—I've decided to rejoin the email group. The main reasons would probably be that I recognize the value in engaging other people along these lines so they can serve as mirrors and because it serves as a reminder to help keep my mind on the problem. For the most part it was more just like things lined up on the side of getting back into the weekly reports.

Much has changed for me in the past several months since leaving the report. V., as you don't know me as I left before you joined the reports, I'll try to give an introduction as well as some idea of where I am now. I've been involved in this sort of thing for about 6 years since starting to attend Art's self-inquiry group in Pittsburgh. I say this sort of thing because along the way my view of what I am involved in has changed. So while from one perspective I could say I have

Epilogues

been searching for self definition for 6 years, it is only more recently that that has become more clearly the problem.

My main concern when I first started this was what I am going to do with my life, which for a long time I associated with finding the perfect career. For the first 5.5 years or so of this I really was going on intellect—afraid of emotions and always trying to work everything out in my head... wanting to have some sort of system of beliefs so that I could know the right answer. During this time I went through many periods of depression, some more severe than others. I was quite a mess during certain periods although there were also times I was riding high when I felt I was living the right life and had thoughts and feelings I approved of very closely associated with that—that I was a seeker (or my idea of what one ought to be, which is how I was trying to answer my lack of identity).

I went through some periods where the thought of spirituality and more ideas made me almost sick, and I ultimately stopped going to meetings and participating in this group because I did not feel hope that it would help me and felt it might even be contributing to my being in my head and my depression. A few months after I stopped these things I went to see a therapist. And working with him helped me a lot—it was like he provided the opposite principle to what I had been thinking, which helped me to get perspective on the whole thing. There were also some significant things that had been coming together in me before seeing him, such as not letting anyone else tell me how I ought to feel or be, etc.... essentially making a big move towards becoming my own authority.

During that time I also started to find something I could rely on in myself—not my thinking, but a feeling to follow inside—and developed some trust in the universe, which I never really had before. With that trust has also come an ability to observe more as I let go more of the notion of control. I have seen with decisions that I am not the one making them, that basically a decision is a process of discovering what I want and once that is discovered, the decision becomes clear. I don't see all decisions this way, but I have seen it with some.

My main complaint nowadays would be being a separate individual—I don't want barriers between me and others—it requires too much energy. My perspective lately has been that it is a lot of work being an individual having to deal with many other individuals. Lately I have just not had much energy—when I have energy, the complaint is more the lack of being one—just the fact of being separate vs. the perceived beauty or happiness of being One and seeing the world as perfect and seeing the world with God's eyes.

※

J. C. continued to live and work in Washington, D.C. The last time I saw him was at a mutual friend's wedding in Pune, India in 2015. Jeff died in July 2018. He and K. P. (see below) had remained close friends since college days at Carnegie Mellon U. In addition to the many, many meetings and retreats we shared, the three of us had made a trip to England to see Douglas Harding in 2004. Kiffy flew into and out of London, while Jeff and I flew into and out of Paris then took the TGV to England. Kiffy and I previously had flown to Las Vegas to attend a gathering of Franklin Merrell-Wolff's students in Lone Pine, CA, and we had made a visit by car to check out Andrew Cohen in Lenox, MA. They were both great travel companions and friends I liked and enjoyed greatly. ~ Art

J. C. and I attended self-inquiry group meetings and weekend retreats in Pittsburgh. He went to CMU at that time. Though he would say he was not in touch with his emotions and lived in his head, i thought he was a sensitive guy. He talked fondly of his family and his grandparents especially. I thought he was really brave as he took up a construction job after graduating from CMU to see how the physical work affects your overall state of mind. I still remember his gentle smiling face. ~ Anima

J. S.
December 2011

I am 52 years old and from D. I am married to P. and we just celebrated 28th anniversary. We have 2 sons, T. 28y and K. 25 y.

I have worked as an OBGYN and subspecialised as a gynecological cancer surgeon. 4½ years ago I decided to walk the Camino, a pilgrimage in Spain. After a few days I got severe endocarditis, and at a certain point in a hospital in Spain, I gave up life. I was simply exhausted by life and did not want to put up with it anymore. I eventually recovered, but it left me with a feeling that I do not want to be here on the conditions that my life had been so far. Looking back, I can see that the feeling had been there for a long time.

I know that it is in deep contrast with the way my life looks from the outside. I have had a lot of success both in my professional and personal life. That is no big help however as it only leaves me with a feeling of bad conscience of not being grateful for all that. I have suffered from severe illness several times in my life, and I have this feeling that it is connected with or is a manifestation of this feeling of life being so strugglesome and heavy. That feeling conflicts with my logic and rational knowing as a doctor. In medical school in D. they do not teach us that disease is caused by feelings, and I am not sure what to think about it myself.

I am longing to live a life that is not so strugglesome. The struggle has something to do with having to contribute to be allowed to be here, so the longing is also for being allowed to be here just because I am. Longing for unconditional love. I have for quite some time known that to find what I long for is a matter of going within, but I also see myself immediately turning my attention outside to find the solution.

I have quit my job ½ year ago. I have been very idealistic trying to help cancer patients, and I have thought I would be able to make a difference. I see it is not possible. There are so many interested parties in health care, so you will always have to make compromises and not just do what is best for the patient. I have spent enough time on that. On the other hand I also want to contribute with all the things I am good at.

For quite some years I have considered leaving my husband. I continually get hurt when he is not able to be there emotionally for me and when he puts things down that are important to me. To me love is about sharing what is important also when you are fumbling to find out what it is. If something is important to me, it does not have to be validated in the outer world to be of value. It is helpful if other people ask questions to help you find out if it is of value or not. For quite some years I have not shared many of my deepest thoughts with him because I do not want them devalued before I am quite sure what they mean to me.

I have been meditating for 9 years. For many years I meditated 2x½ hour daily and I have been to many retreats meditating for many hours. It is called Acem meditation and is effortless meditation with a mantra. After long meditations, we talk about our meditations in guidance groups. I also teach meditation and lead guidance groups. Meditation for me has been very helpful. From the very first day I felt I had ½ hour free from my thoughts telling me that I did this and that wrong and that I am not very good at whatever. The thoughts were still there, but I did not have to pay attention or argue with them. That was a big relief. Over the years there are not as many of those thoughts. It has also taught me to be alone with myself and enjoy the company. ☺ Through meditation and guidance groups I have worked through a lot of psychological stuff from my life. The last years I have not been meditating regularly and have a feeling that it does not take me any further.

I have heard about TAT from my son T. and came over for the April TAT meeting 2011, and I just got back from a longer stay in the US. I was in solitude in Pittsburgh for two weeks and went to a 5-day retreat led by Art Ticknor and ended my stay at the TAT November meeting at Penn Scenic View. I had a very inspiring journey, but I am back to everyday life again. It took 5 days before it struck after I got back. ☺

Objective for the retreat in Nov:

- To cast the illusion that I find freedom in the outer world. Become more familiar with my inner voice, intuition and trust it.
- Spend time with friends that are familiar with self inquiry to find out what it is ☺ and explore the potential for me.

I have not at all digested all the impressions from my journey, but attending this email group is part of my strategy to keep myself focused. I have the time to work on my spiritual path, but I am also very good at distracting myself.

※

J. S. died in January 2019. She was in an online confrontation group with me. I found her to be self-honest about her life and herself. She asked herself and others questions that make you reevaluate your motives. ~ Anima

The last time I saw J. S. was when she invited Bob F., Nina S. and myself to stay at her house when we took a whirlwind tour of Europe after a 2012 retreat that Tess Hughes hosted in Galway, Ireland that Bob and I assisted with and that J. S. attended. She and her family were gracious hosts. She was a very intelligent and sensitive person and, although we weren't close friends, I have fond memories of her. ~ Art

K. P.
September 2005
My job, for the time being, has all but taken over my life. Yes, I have free time, but today, for instance, out of a day of 15 hours, I worked for about 13. Now, working means a lot of things—being at football practice, eating dinner with the kids in a formal setting, attending meetings, etc., so it is not as though I'm at the grindstone 24/7, but the truth is that I also have very little free time right now. I am waiting to see what happens once I've been at this for a while, but it already seems clear that I will not be back here at K. [a private prep boarding school where he was teaching] next year because I have no desire to give two to three hours each day towards high school athletic practice. There are a lot of teaching jobs where such would not be part of the requirement.

I will try to get around to doing the report better come this weekend. Last weekend I was in Buffalo with the football team, leaving K. at 5 pm Friday and coming back at 11 pm Saturday. Sunday was spent almost entirely on work related stuff. I am okay with it for now, but probably mostly because I am under the impression that it will calm down once I have my mind around the practical side of things better.

Epilogues

K. P. later earned an MBA, married, became a parent, worked as a consultant for a top management consulting firm, and then as a project leader for a major multinational technology company. He died in April 2020. I hadn't heard much from K. P. after 2007, although I recall an email where he said that the great lesson he learned from his association with TAT was the value of friendship. Along the lines I mentioned in my comment on JC above, they were both friends I admired and have many fond memories of. ~ Art

I knew K. P. when he was a student at CMU. He came to the Monday self-inquiry group meetings and also would come to weekend retreats. Out of all the students who were coming regularly to the meetings, I thought Kiffy was most friendly and approachable. I still remember him playing with two month old Meera(my daughter) and me thinking "I hope he doesn't drop her" since she was almost upside down on his raised legs…:) ~ Anima

My Story

Anima
\# December 2011

I was born in a small town, Dehradun, in India. Lived with my maternal grandparents for the first four years of my life since my mom was going to school getting her teaching degree.

Life, growing up, was simple and very seasonal. Everyone in our little village, Kanwali, had the same last name. My dad was a farmer. We lived in our ancestral home with extended family. There were lots of cousins and aunts and uncles. Alcohol, I thought was a norm because I saw most men drinking in our village. My dad was an alcoholic, which I did not understand was a disease. It affected our family in all aspects. I grew up feeling constantly worried about him, my mother and my younger siblings. I rarely saw him sober.

One fine day, his body just gave up... he got really sick. That was the turning point for him as well as for us. He turned towards spirituality. He started meditating and turned to Osho's group. That influenced me as well. He constantly told us to watch and be aware of who was looking. This got me in the habit of watching my thoughts and my actions. It almost felt like I was split into two... one acting and one watching.

As a child I remember feeling that this was all a dream and I was someplace else dreaming this life. Being born in a Hindu household, there are certain beliefs that are just part of who you are...for example, reincarnation; God is all there is, in everything, has no shape but will appear in whatever form I would imagine him as. So, as a child, in times of crisis

Epilogues

I would turn to my personal God in the form of Krishna. My miserable inner life made me focus on something bigger than my environment. I started meditating when I was in my late teens. My grandfather had a big collection of spiritual/philosophical books that I thought was a treasure. My dad was reading Osho. Although most of the time I, being the annoying teenager, rebelled and questioned whatever my dad said.

I know it impacted my thinking. Looking back, I am surprised that my dad encouraged questioning from us. He was quite open-minded and let me make my decisions.

Sharad and I got married and moved to Pittsburgh in August of 1998. This is when I discovered the Philosophical Self-Inquiry (PSI) group that I feel changed my life. I was dealing with my dad's death, just being married, and not knowing what or where my life was going. I felt completely lost then.

Saw a flyer in the library about 'What are your goals in life?' I thought it was one of those career-related seminars that help you sort out your mess. Went to the meeting on Monday and met Art, Cecy and Reggie there. Found myself saying that the purpose of my life was to find enlightenment.

After that first meeting, nothing could keep me away from being part of this group of seekers. Felt really happy because it was just so honest and I could talk about the most important aspects of my life without getting preached or judged. Going to these meetings was like psychotherapy for me. Initially this group or Mr. Rose's approach did not fit into my picture of a 'spiritual' group as there were no incense sticks, guru in white/saffron robes or holier-than-thou pure people. It was a period of insights and realizations into my psychology. My focus shifted from outside to completely inwards. I know if I hadn't met Art that day... my life would have been going in a totally different direction today. Mr.

Rose said that psychology and spirituality go hand in hand. It is really true for me.

Self-inquiry started as trying to understand this little-s self first. It was hard for me to accept the robotic nature of this little being, 'anima'. I eventually came to a point where I realized I was done with the psychological work, there was nothing more I could do about my personality, and there really was no path. God had to be here and now, not in some distant future. The problem was somehow this little 'me' getting in the way. But how does one get itself out of the way?

I used to think that having a family (kids) would be the biggest block in my spiritual search. But as I was getting into my thirties, I realized that nature would not stop bothering me if I didn't get done with what it expected me to do... that is, to have children. Got pregnant... and that was the period where I got to observe my physical body closely. I could see how everything about this anima was at the physical level... all the desires, idiosyncrasies, the special little things that we get so identified with, etc., were totally at this physical level. Little self just simply dissipated as I observed. Little anima was just a simple robot going about mundane life, doing the habitual stuff, thinking the thoughts and just existing. Pretty soon even the desire for enlightenment disappeared as it felt it was only for ego gratification. There really was nobody in the driver's seat. The vehicle moved quite efficiently on its own. The self had disappeared completely, at least that is how it felt.

Then in May 2004, Art, on a solitary retreat, had a breakthrough. When I heard about it, it was the happiest day of my life. I thought this is my chance to talk to God directly. On June 03, 2004, I was unable to sleep. It was 5.30 in the morning. The thought occurred 'I wonder what God feels like' and in that moment I witnessed/experienced what Wren-Lewis describes as 'Dazzling Darkness'. If you can imagine

Epilogues

what Alive Energy would feel like, It was That. The physical body-and-mind was lying on the bed just panicking. Head felt it was about to burst, the blood was simply rushing to the head, eyes were watering and mind was having thoughts... there were no eyes needed to see It, or ears to hear It, or any of the tools that we have to Be It.... I was/am That.... Physical body/mind wanted to turn away from the experience because it wasn't comfortable and there was a feeling that body would die if consciousness would not return.

I realized that I am the Absolute, non individualized Awareness, and so is everything else. The little woman (as Bob F. calls it) still goes on playing its role but with that complete Freedom which you will understand one day.

Interview with Anima
Mario Pallua, 2011-08-16

1. What was your life like prior to starting seeking?

I can't remember if I ever started seeking with an intention. When I was twelve, I learned meditation in a yoga class that my dad had enrolled us in. Meditation was an escape from my life. Growing up in an environment infused with alcohol addiction really shapes all aspects of human life. I remember feeling anxious and worried all the time for my parents and my siblings. I saw life to be a burden, not only mine but everybody else's around me.

During one of the Osho retreats that I went to, I realized that I was the observer of my life. Noticing that I was the observer and not the actor brought a little distance from 'my life story'. It was like a switch that got flicked. My identity shifted from this sufferer of life to an observer of life.

Life otherwise was school, friends, career, and the dream of 'I will be happy one day'.

2. What got you interested in seeking?

Life. I don't see that I deliberately chose to be interested. Nothing else in life appealed in that permanent, long term sense. Of course, there were temporary fascinations that appeared and disappeared. It was when my dad passed away that I realized I was completely lost. It was like hitting rock bottom. When you are drowning, you will catch hold of any log that you find floating by. Coming across the PSI group in Pittsburgh is what gave me a clear purpose and direction.

3. As seekers, we often notice, but cannot get over our delusions or beliefs. Were there any particularly traumatic or funny ones that stood out on your path?

The belief that I was a special, separate, suffering, human being. The belief that the reason for my suffering lay in the universe outside. It took a lot of slaps from life for me to admit that no matter what is going on inside or outside, I am the one who is responsible for everything that is manifesting as my life. The belief that Sharad, my husband, will become what I expect him to be, and then we will live happily ever after. (This is my secret life project and I am still working on it...:-))

4. During your seeking, what did you think the path was all about?

The path was about not facing your immediate suffering and turning your attention to something beyond. I thought the path would bring eternal peace and happiness based on my definition of what peace and happiness meant.

5. Looking back, what would you say the path is all about? What is the work that is to be done? Can we gauge progress?

The path is one of subtraction. When you realize that it is 'you' that is in the way, the real work starts. It is not possible for ego to catch and eliminate itself. The process of 'self-observation' does shrink the self/ego though.

Progress is when you realize that no matter how much you fine-tune the mind or the technique, it all feeds the individual I-sense. Ego maintains its centricity.

I figured that the only way to deal with the ego was by becoming indifferent to everything that was perceived as ego enhancers. The story of suffering and seeking also got dropped. Progress is the purification of your desire for Truth.

6. What advice would you give out to someone just starting on the path?

I will give the advice that was most astute for me: become a scientist and study yourself. For this, I had to first learn to be a scientist. To maintain objectivity based on facts and what is observed, vs. your personal preferences.

7. Some teachers say it's all quite simple and obvious, which we today know best as the neo-advaita. What is your view on this type of teaching?

Yes. This is the Truth. But does it help you as a seeker?

8. Were you changed by the path, by the final event, or both? What happened to your suffering?

The simple process of self-observation and inquiring why and where is the shoe pinching, helps in cleaning out the clutter. Brings clarity. Everything that I thought I would find if I got enlightened came much before. My understanding or definition of objects changed.

The organism does reach its highest potential of being. Old habits and complaints serve as a source of engagement. There seems to be access to direct knowledge of what is in front.

My understanding of what is suffering and who is suffering changed when I inquired into the nature of suffering and the sufferer.

9. As a seeker, you were emotional or rational? Is one more useful than the other?

Emotional. Being emotional or feelings-driven felt more natural. Maybe because I am a woman. Emotions usually underlie how life gets lived even when you see yourself as intellect-driven. The problem arises when you notice how quickly emotions change. In a short span of time, you realize your perspective feels completely contradictory to what it was a few moments before.

To live a sane life, you need to have both your emotional and logical muscles strong.

10. What is the method of confrontation all about?

Confrontation, I found, was the best practice that worked for me. The mind became completely serious when a question was posed. Even when the answer didn't become clear right away, the mind chewed on the problem until clarity was found.

Confrontation in its essence is the process of holding the mirror for your fellow seeker with the hope of helping them see some underlying belief they have about themselves.

It is an intentional affliction to the ego with the hope of seeing the underlying belief that keeps the attention on it.

11. What do you know for sure? What is enlightenment? Are you sure?

Enlightenment is the realization of who you are.

There are no questions or doubts left that require assurance or proof.

12. What is death?

It is an end to a beginning.

13. What are you?

You and I are not two.

14. Why do you teach? How do you teach?

No, I do not teach. I can only share my experience and what I found with other beings who are still suffering.

15. What would you say to a seeker who despairs of ever finding what she's looking for?

What you are seeking is not creating obstacles for you. Your limitations are coming from your beliefs about yourself. Who is this that will find or not find the answer? How is ego/you getting compensated for having this belief?

16. What/where is the truth? Is it far away?

If Truth is an object then of course it has to be in time and space. Two objects have a spatial relationship. So the correct question would be where are you in relation to the Truth.
    Truth is all there is. There is nothing else but Truth.

Rice Cakes

The spiritual path is not about perfecting ourselves (ain't gonna happen :-). The purification that occurs is one of dropping pretenses about what we are... or more accurately, pretenses drop as we see through them. Like kids losing interest in toys. Or the child seeing that its mother isn't an angel of perfection but a human being with human characteristics.

Ego is based on the conviction of being an individual something, and that conviction begins to break down when we realize we're "nothing special." Specialness depends on difference, which means having characteristics that are superior or inferior. Egoism and an inflated sense of self, either positive or negative, go hand in hand.

There's no fix for personality. The cure is to take the focus off personality and turn it to awareness.

That which experiences has no parts, is whole and complete. We don't find it *in* experience.

Self-consciousness is the sleepwalker's clue of where to look to find the Real self. The opening of the proverbial third eye may point to psychic input, but it may also point to a more conscious stage of the mind's being able to look back at what we're looking out from.

❧

Productive self-questioning or self-inquiry doesn't produce good or right answers but stimulates the mind to look within. The intellect serves up warmed-over responses. It's a tertiary process. It works with the pretense of knowing. True self-questioning relies on doubt, which generates looking (if we don't turn away in fear or pride), which generates feelings, which generates conceptual thoughts.

❧

If thinking gets in the way of observing, stop thinking.

❧

The mind receives and projects. What-you-are observes.

❧

When you get a clear sighting of your #1 priority, it will automatically become your life's commitment, and all the lesser-priority things will take care of themselves.

❧

Epilogues

Spiritual progress occurs by dispelling illusory beliefs and is thus a subtractive business. The end result of spiritual investigation is knowing what we are at the core of our being. This knowing is not a type of knowing we're familiar with since it goes beyond the knower/known split. We recognize our essential nature by becoming one with it. The drop of rain loses its boundaries, its individuality, when it hits the ocean.

~ Art

Interview with Art
Mario Pallua, 2011-08-16

What was your life like prior to starting seeking?

What I'd describe generously as semi-conscious seeking began when I "woke up" as a college senior to the boring prospect of working an 8 to 5 job five days a week for the foreseeable decades. Over the next 10 or 12 years I experienced periodic identity crises, as I thought of them, where I'd be flooded by feelings that my life was missing some purpose or meaning. But I would scan the horizon for what might fill that hole, and nothing that I could conceive of sounded satisfying.

What got you interested in seeking?

My wife and I had taken our kids to the local library one rainy Sunday, and she spotted a poster that she thought I'd be interested in. It was for a Zen group meeting at the local university. It took a full year before I finally got to one of their weekly meetings, which took place when classes were in session during the fall, spring and winter academic quarters. The group had formed when Richard Rose gave a public talk at the university a few years earlier. When he attended a meeting several months after I became a regular participant, he rang an inner bell I didn't know even existed. I credit that bell-ringing with an awakening of my intuition to the prospect of finding what I was looking for, within.

Epilogues

As seekers, we often notice, but cannot get over our delusions or beliefs. Were there any particularly traumatic or funny ones that stood out on your path?

As Charlie Chaplin was quoted as saying, life is a tragedy in close-up and a comedy in far shot. When I was seeking to find my true or real self, I was pretty much stuck in close-up. Every illusion or delusion that got popped lifted a weight from me, but I don't recall any that were particularly traumatic or funny. I was a rationalist, though, and thought feelings were something to deal with (as opposed to something simply to feel), so I'm sure that helped obscure the reactions I felt to those belief balloons popping.

During your seeking, what did you think the path was all about?

I was tremendously fortunate in having a teacher who'd been all the way down the path, so I didn't have any pie-in-the-sky fantasies about the path. I knew it would take determined effort with no guaranteed payoff. But I also felt rather sure that I would not regret a life dedicated to searching for my real self regardless of whether the search proved successful.

Looking back, what would you say the path is all about? What is the work that is to be done? Can we gauge progress?

I'd say that the path to Self or Truth or Reality is subtractive, shaking off or seeing through faulty beliefs that obscure the truth or prevent us from accepting the truth that is always in plain view. Those faulty self-beliefs keep us asleep to the truth. The work is to wake up. There are a few discontinuities along the way that we see in retrospect as milestones. While we're on the path, though, it's difficult to gauge progress. After 25 years of effort I went through a period of feeling like I was right back where I'd started. Fortunately I had some friends whom I was working with who could provide contradictory views.

What advice would you give out to someone just starting on the path?

The only thing I can say for sure that's needed is determination to keep going even though there will likely be periods, maybe lengthy ones, of discouragement. And then keep going even when you get to the point of seeing there's nothing in it for you.

Some teachers say it's all quite simple and obvious, which we today know best as the neo-advaita. What is your view on this type of teaching?

Any belief is a potential trap.

Was Art changed by the path, by the final event, or both? What happened to your suffering?

Art's pretty much the same, although he can afford to feel his feelings deeply these days since there's no threat of extinction hanging over his head. He knows that he never really existed :-). He's still programmed to continue existing, though, and possibly every cell of his body shares that programming. Art—the body-mind self—still feels pain and pleasure. I am beyond or before or behind movement. There's no suffering where I am.

Epilogues

You often mention that as a seeker you were more linear, logical, rational. Looking back, what is the place of rationality on the path?

Most seekers, I suspect, lean either toward feeling or toward rational thought as their weapon of choice to try to get what they want from the world. Franklin Merrell-Wolff, a very rational guy, concluded that Buddha was the world-class teacher who had been the most balanced between the two extremes as a seeker, while Jesus was primarily on the feeling side and Shankara primarily on the thinking side. Using both thought and feeling would be great, but I suspect that most of us will stay pretty much in one rut or the other for most of our seeking. Intuition is what I believe determines progress. Intuition shows up somewhat differently in feelers and in thinkers. My advice would be for thinkers not to be afraid of intuition and for feelers not to believe all feelings are intuition.

You are known for your skills in seeing the blocks of seekers and confronting them without too much fuss. What is the method of confrontation all about?

The best confrontation is self-questioning. Our faulty beliefs mostly fly under our radar, so it's hard for us to get them into view for questioning. Working with friends can accelerate the process. Most of the helpful confrontation probably occurs by accident.

What do you know for sure? What is enlightenment? Are you sure?

The only thing I know for sure is what I am. Enlightenment is an open channel between the self-conscious mind and Awareness. The individual self of the body-mind recognizes that its existence, as the word literally means, is a "standing outside of" its core being.

What is death?

Human death is like a faster version of the death of a boulder.

What are you?

I am your "original face" before you were born.

Why do you teach? How do you teach?

I'll take refuge in what Richard Rose said when I asked him that question: "I can't help myself... it's an obsession." He had a dry sense of humor that I've never seen surpassed. The best explanation I can come up with is the same thing that seemed to move me along the path: momentum. I started leaning in a direction and couldn't stop. My attempts to help other seekers seem to be more of the same: stumbling along in the hopes that something will work. Another, prettier, description might be: faith. A more vanilla description might be: it's what Art's programmed to do.

What would you say to a seeker that despairs of ever finding what she's looking for?

That's a good position to be in... as long as you keep on with the quest. Working without any hope of reward is the final stage of the path. Be thankful if it's quick or easy, but don't expect it to be.

What/where is the truth? Is it far away?

The Truth is that which is beyond reach by any except itself.

They Are Not Long
Ernest Dowson (1867-1900)

They are not long, the weeping and the laughter,
Love and desire and hate:
I think they have no portion in us after
We pass the gate.

They are not long, the days of wine and roses:
Out of a misty dream
Our path emerges for a while, then closes
Within a dream.

Final Thoughts

Art / What I've Learned of Love

*P*ersonal love:
1. Comes and goes
2. Wanting to become one with
3. Teaches us through emotional ups and downs
4. There's always more to learn

Impersonal love:
1. The core of being
2. The from and to of existence
3. Timeless, spaceless, never-changing perfection

※

Anima / A Love Story

ॐ पूर्णमदः पूर्णमिदं पूर्णात्पुर्णमुदच्यते
पूर्णश्य पूर्णमादाय पूर्णमेवावशष्यिते ॥
ॐ शान्तिः शान्तिः शान्तिः ॥

Om Puurnnam-Adah Puurnnam-Idam Puurnnaat-Purnnam-Udacyate
Puurnnashya Puurnnam-Aadaaya Puurnnam-Eva-Avashissyate ||
Om Shaantih Shaantih Shaantih ||

This is whole; That is whole.
From That (unmanifest) wholeness,
This wholeness (manifestation) comes.
Taking away the whole
From the whole,
The whole remains.
Om Peace Peace Peace

This is the Shanti Mantra from the *Isha Upanishad*.[86] I had known this mantra for a long time without really understanding it. One Sunday morning I had taken my kids to the temple for their Hindi language class. While they had the class, in the main hall, Acharyaji[87] was giving some discourse that I wasn't paying much attention to. My wandering mind noticed that on the ceiling of the hall, there were mantras and the meaning of the mantras inscribed.

That day when I read this Shanti mantra and the meaning, I got goosebumps. With what clarity a fellow human, only a few thousand years ago, had found words to describe the indescribable.

This is my favorite love song.

---

86 The *Upanishads* are late Vedic Sanskrit texts of religious teaching and ideas still revered in Hinduism.
87 Head priest/teacher.

Index

A

About the Authors 3
A Change of Heart 270
A Letter to My Younger
    Self 267
Always Right Behind You
    21, 281
And God Smiled 132
An Interesting Dream 265
Apple Tree 36
Are You a Robot? 203
Are You Free? 300
A Simple Formula 25
A Wave of Timelessness
    197, 350

B

Bhagwan's Love 232
Buddha Nature 179, 350
Burning Intensity 308

C

Capacity to Love 224
Complete Surrender 186
Craving, Longing,
    Yearning 189
Credo 298

D

Dead Particles 166
Dear Friend 283, 303
Decalogue 37
Desire vs. Longing 81, 350
Direct Experience 31, 145
Does the Mind See 138
Dream Comfort 76

E

Elusion 167, 350
Emotions 192, 332
Enlightenment Holds 71
Evolution of a Seeker 142

F

Facing Fear & Depression
    116
Falling in Love 214
Feedback to Art 89
Feelings About Love 226,
    350
Feet of Clay 169
Final Thoughts 344
First Glimpse of Home 103
Freedom 101, 124, 127, 145,
    217, 268, 295, 328
Full Moon 276
Futility of Love 222

G

Gayatri Mantra *15*
Giridhar Is My True Love *236, 351*
Going Home *255*
Gurus *17*
Guru-Shishya *33*

H

Hearing *156, 290*
Hey, Girlfriend *244*
Homage to Love *168*
How Do You Relate to Me *165*

I

I Believe That *114*
I Don't Get It *98*
In Memoriam *86*
Interview with Anima *329, 351*
Interview with Art *337, 351*
Is It Worth It *45*
I Who Speak *309, 351*

L

Let Death Be Your Teacher *104*
Letter to God *271, 351*
Longing *46, 81, 189, 321, 350*
Loss of Everything *193*
Loss of Self *160*
Love Is Simple *67*
Love's Response *239*

M

Maniram's Pets *155*
Man Reads a Book *302*
Monody *57, 350*
Mr. Wetherill *218*
My Story *325*

N

Nature *68, 89, 179, 183, 245, 350*
No Room *194*
Nostalgia *128, 192*
Notes from a 1981 Winter Intensive *83*
Nothing and Everything *301*
Nuts and Bolts *119*

O

Only *94, 173, 195, 292*
Opening a Path *23, 350*
Opening Your Heart *107*
Ordinary People *59*
Overwhelmed *107, 140*

P

Pass It On *78*
Peace Prayer *225, 350*
Poison Ivy *47*
Process Observer *152, 205, 206*
Productive Mood *170*
Profound Writings, East & West *241*

Promise 154
Purpose and Benefit 172
Pursuit of Relentless Love 231

Q

Questions Answered 284
Questions from Mark 26

R

Rapport 109
Renouncing Maya 43
Reviews, Pertinent and Impertinent 6
Rice Cakes 334
Roadmap of My Inner Path 291

S

Sahajo Bai 216
Salvation 112
Seeing What You're Looking Out From 205
Seekers' Stories from Friends Who Have Passed 312
Self-Definition 150
Separation Anxiety 49
Seriously 53
Shades of Gray 58
Show Me How 261, 351
Sikhism 93

Silence 113
Slippery Eel 147
Strategy 95
Struggling Blindly 92
Stumbling into Love 90, 234
Svetaketu 249

T

Teacher Criteria 80
The Ascent of Mount Carmel 69, 350
The Bhakti Doorway 278
The Dreamer 306
The Ego 162
The Horse Is Out 44
The Love Beyond Love 70
The Nature of Desire 183
The No-Head Circle 287
The "NO" Poem 310
The Paradox of Acceptance 253
The Problem's Not in the Transmission 200
The Purpose of Life 305
The Summer of 1998 18
They Are Not Long 343, 351
Thy Will 74, 75, 94
Time Capsule 99
Tough Love 174
Triangulation 194, 263
True Love 236, 273, 279

Turning Attention from
   Not-Self *130*

U

Understanding the Mind
   190
Uninvited Guest *221, 239*
Unity *195, 241, 279*

W

Wakil's Dream *90*
What Do I Know of Love
   220
What Seekers Can Learn
   from *93*
What Tool to Use *82*
When Confrontation
   Works *110*
When Flame Was a Flower
   176
Where Is the Path *180*
Whirlwind *198*
Why Stories *39*
Witnessing Death *50*

Credits & Permissions

About the Authors
Chuck W. note of thanks
Photo of Anima and Art - *retreat participant*

Chapter 1: Where to Begin
"Opening a Path" - *Shawn Nevins*
Painting - *Zen Master Hakuin / Public Domain*

Chapter 2: Suffering
Renounce Maya - *Kabir / Public Domain*
Longing - *Ben Rainey*
Monody - *Herman Melville / Public Domain*
The Ascent of Mount Carmel - *St. John of the Cross / Public Domain*

Chapter 3: Walking the Path
Desire vs. Longing - *Dan McLaughlin*

Chapter 4: Self-Inquiry: What Is the Practice?

Chapter 5: Identity: Who Am I?
Elusion - *Corina Bardasuc*

Chapter 6: Is There an End?
Buddha Nature - *Richard Rose / Fair Use*
A Wave of Timelessness - *M K Rawlings / Public Domain*

Chapter 7: Colors of Love
Peace Prayer - *St. Francis of Assisi / Public Domain*
Feelings About Love - *Men's retreat participants*
Giridhar Is My True Love - *Meera Bai / Public Domain*

Chapter 8: Tales, East & West
Show Me How - *William Samuel / Sandy Jones*
Letter to God - *Ricky Cobb III*

Chapter 9: And In The End
No-Head Circle drawing - *Douglas Harding / Richard Lang*
I Who Speak - *Franklin Merrell-Wolff / Doroethy Leonard*

10. Epilogues
An Interview with Anima - *Mario Pallua*
An Interview with Art - *Mario Pallua*
They Are Not Long - *Ernest Dowson / Public Domain*

Other Titles from TAT Foundation Press

Sense of Self: The Source of All Existential Suffering?
by Art Ticknor

Hydroglyphics: Reflections on the Sacred
by Phaedra Greenwood and Shawn Nevins

Falling For Truth: A Spiritual Death And Awakening
by Howdie Mickoski

Awake at the Wheel: Norio Kushi's Highway Adventures and the Unmasking of the Phantom Self by Stephen Earle

Subtraction: The Simple Math of Enlightenment
by Shawn Nevins

This Above All: A Journey of Self-Discovery
by Tess Hughes

A Handyman's Common Sense Guide to Spiritual Seeking
by David Weimer

At Home with the Inner Self
by Jim Burns

Beyond Mind, Beyond Death

Beyond Relativity: Transcending the Split Between Knower & Known by Art Ticknor

The Celibate Seeker by Shawn Nevins

Images of Essence by Bob Fergeson and Shawn Nevins

The Listening Attention by Bob Fergeson

The Perennial Way: New English versions of Yoga Sutras, Dhammapada, Heart Sutra, Ashtavakra Gita, Faith Mind Sutra, and Tao Te Ching by Bart Marshall

Solid Ground of Being: A Personal Story of the Impersonal by Art Ticknor

For more information on the TAT Foundation visit tatfoundation.org.

Made in the USA
Monee, IL
15 February 2022